The Photographer's Quick Guide To

Earning Money From YOUR Photos

KIM LAMBERT

KIM LAMBERT

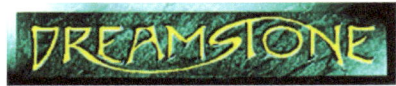

Published by Dreamstone © 2014

www.dreamstone.com.au

Copyright © 2014 Kim Lambert

All rights reserved.

ISBN: 1925165019

ISBN-13: 978-1-925165-01-2

Cover image and all images in this book © Kim Lambert
Except – Portrait of Kim Lambert © Tomasz Ciolek

The Photographer's Quick Guide to Earning Money From Your Photos

The "Photographer's Quick Guide.." Series

By Kim Lambert

- Earning Money from Your Photos
- Taking Beautiful Portraits
- Taking Spectacular Travel photos
- Capturing Amazing Landscapes
- Getting Up Close – Macro Photos
- Urban and Industrial Photography
- Pictures with a Holiday Theme
- Taking Great Pictures of People
- Taking Gorgeous Food Photos
- Publishing Books with Your Pictures
- Finding Local Places to Sell Your Prints
- Selling Your Photos Online
- Tying it all Together: Actively Marketing Your Photography

All Books will be available from all Amazon sites and other book stores, and available for Kindle too!

Watch out for each title as it is released

KIM LAMBERT

Thank You For Buying This Book !

I hope that you enjoy it (and the many spectacular photos that you take).

May your photos contribute to your cash flow from now on!

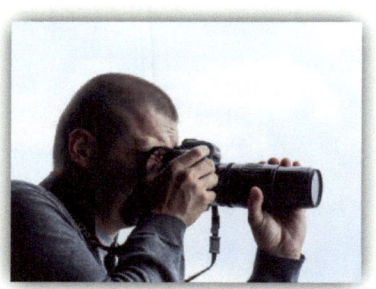

Please leave us a review on Amazon and let us know !

The Photographer's Quick Guide to Earning Money From Your Photos

Disclaimer

All photography is an experiment in a sense, and many people will take photos of the same places or things over time. All photos in this book are the author's, or the photographer's herein attributed, and should any bear a close resemblance to those used elsewhere, that is purely coincidental.

Whilst the content of this book presents the author's best knowledge on the subject of ways to earn money from your photography, no earnings guarantees are suggested or made, no financial advice is offered – this information is purely educational and should be used as you personally choose, after consultation with appropriate professionals.

© Kim Lambert 2014, all rights reserved.

No parts of this work may be copied without the authors permission.

If you would like to provide feedback on this book please send it to info@dreamstone.com.au

KIM LAMBERT

Table of Contents

Disclaimer v

What Readers are Saying About this Book, and Others in the Series viii

Acknowledgements ix

Preface xi

Foreword xiii

How to use this book - What this series is about xvi

Introduction xvii

Chapter 1 - 4 Key Things That Make a Picture '"Money Worthy" - Regardless of Where You Sell It 1

Chapter 2 - 8 Places/Ways You Can Sell Your Photos 15

The Photographer's Quick Guide to Earning Money From Your Photos

Chapter 3 - 9 Common Mistakes That Can Stop You From Making Money With Your Photos 35

Chapter 4 - 12 Different Kinds of Photography You Can Make Money From 51

Chapter 5 - Debunking Common Myths About Making Money From Photography 73

Chapter 6 - Your Action Plan 79

Chapter 7 - Resource Lists 85

Look out for further titles in The "Photographer's Quick Guide.." Series 91

Other Books from Dreamstone Publishing 92

ABOUT THE AUTHOR 93

KIM LAMBERT

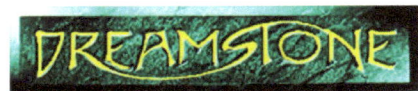

What Readers are Saying About this Book, and Others in the Series

"The Photographers Quick Guide to Earning Money From Your Photos" is a great, simple and a concise guide for those of us who want to make some (or a lot) of extra cash from our photos. This book is packed with well explained examples and provides a great list of the the "do's" and the "dont's" of how to go about it all. As a bonus, there is a resource section to help you get going as soon as, if not before, you have finished reading the whole book.

Tomasz Ciolek - Photographer, IT security specialist, geek.

Acknowledgements

Thanks to all those photographers whose work inspired us to create photos of our own with the same sort of look and feel, or to visit amazing and unusual places, just to photograph them – you are a source of ongoing inspiration.

Thanks also to the team at Great Escape Publishing and The Photographers Life website (see resource list in Chapter 7), for your support and your great courses.

KIM LAMBERT

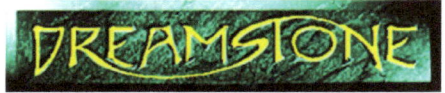

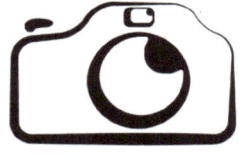

The Photographer's Quick Guide to Earning Money From Your Photos

Preface

Enjoy Using This Book !

This book is designed to make it easy, and enjoyable, to take amazing, beautiful, high quality photographs, and present them in beautiful, decorative and inventive ways, that will make everyone who sees them impressed with your photography skills, as well as allowing you to earn money from your photos, in a multitude of ways!.

Have Fun !

KIM LAMBERT

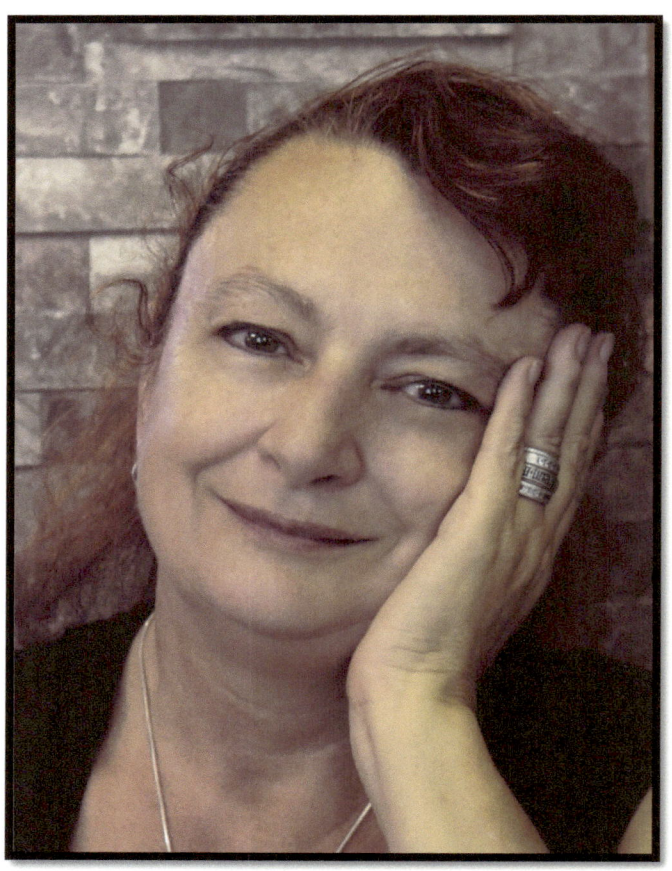

(Photo – Tomasz Ciolek)

The Photographer's Quick Guide to Earning Money From Your Photos

Foreword

So, why am I writing these books ? Here is a little about my photographic history, and how it lead to here.

Photography seems to have been a significant part of my life at all times. My parents had cameras (multiple), and took many photos, in an era where that was not all that common. They therefore got me a basic camera as soon as I showed any interest at all. As a small child I took pretty terrible pictures (as do most small children) but by the time I was 15 I was taking quite good shots of fairly difficult subjects (like fast moving horses over jumps) well enough to have a few of them published with small articles in magazines.

It seemed inevitable that I would end up with others around me with similar interests, and my photographic knowledge got expanded by one of my first boyfriends, who had a full darkroom setup (albeit intermittent, as it happened in his parent's bathroom!) and did some professional work as a sideline. A few years later I found myself working as a professional photographer and spent some years doing everything from school portraits to weddings and debutante balls.

I decided that I was not exactly thrilled with that as a job - whilst I enjoy capturing the essence of a subject in a portrait, I prefer to do that with time to spare rather than in formal conditions with stressed subjects.

KIM LAMBERT

So, after a short burst of working in other industries, I found myself drawn back into photography, this time managing retail camera stores. In general I enjoyed this, and it not only gave me an extended range of knowledge of camera equipment and use, but a growing understanding of how little most people knew on the topic, and how often people did not have a try at doing what they wanted to with photography, because they felt that it was "all too hard".

I then went on to work in many other areas, progressively more centered in Computers and IT, but the interest in photography stayed with me, and those I associated with all tended to be interested in, and have worked in, the photographic field, in one area or another. As digital cameras became available, I was very aware of the possibilities, and closely associated with those using, for business, some of the earliest ones on the market.

Once high quality mass market small size digital cameras became commonplace, I began to take a lot of photos again. I have done a lot of outdoors activities, and travelled quite a lot in my life, and this has made me very aware of all of the beautiful things around me. I have never lost the habit of mentally framing them to a picture, even if I do not have a camera to hand.

Small digital cameras removed the cost limitation of film - I have always believed the adage that, to get a good shot you have to take lots of photos - 1 in 10 will be worthwhile. So now I have the ability to capture all of those things that I framed in my mind, to always carry a camera with me, and to show to others the detail in my world, which more and more fascinates me in its beauty and diversity.

The Photographer's Quick Guide to Earning Money From Your Photos

I have previously produced a number of photo books (such as "Detailed Beauty : Australia Through the Macro Lens", which is currently available at Blurb.com), and the majority of the photos used in these "Photographer's Quick Guide " books are drawn from my personal catalog of more than 100,000 digital photos (a count which grows every day, at a pretty rapid rate!).

I dedicate this book series to making photography accessible and easy for people with ordinary digital cameras, with no need for deep technical knowledge of any kind.

These books will help you take better photos, and make money from them, should you choose to do so, in whatever areas appeal to you.

Kim Lambert

2014

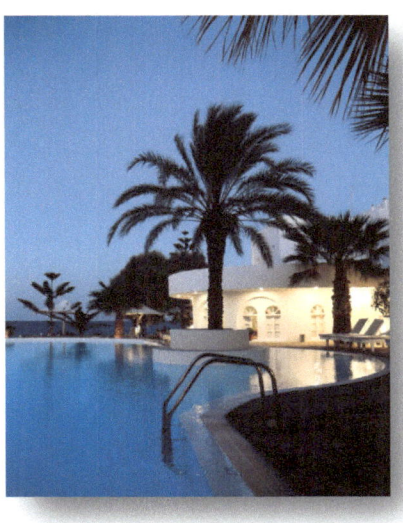

KIM LAMBERT

How to Use This Book – What This Series is About

This series is aimed at being exactly what the title says – a set of Photographer's "Quick Guides" – each book covers some key points associated with just one photography topic – be that how to take a certain type of photo, or how to sell your photos in a certain way.

The books are designed to be used as quick references, to get you started in a particular area. Each also includes a Resources section, that provides information on things discussed in the book, and places where you can go to learn much more on particular topics, if you want to dive deeper.

So, whether you carry the guides with you on a Kindle, an Ipad, a tablet, a smartphone or in paperback form, they are there to give you hints and reminders as you go, about all the key things that will make your photos better, and more saleable, regardless of what you photograph!

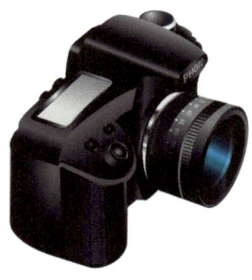

The Photographer's Quick Guide to Earning Money From Your Photos

Introduction

This Quick Guide is about Earning Money From Your Photos. Like all of the Guide's it is focused on providing you with quality information on just one topic area of photography.

The aim of each book is to cover key information on that topic – Dos, don'ts, methods, markets and relevant resources. This first Guide, being focused on earning money from your photography, is somewhat broader in scope than most of the others, but aims to prepare you for making your photos pay, no matter what other areas you may choose to pursue. This Guide covers a wide range of places that you can sell your work, with hints on how to make your pictures "money worthy" regardless of where you want to sell them

The Guides may be read in sequence, or individually – each stands alone, but together they become a comprehensive reference set for any photographer.

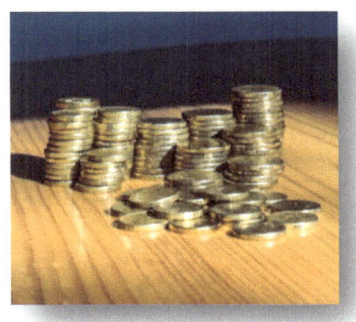

KIM LAMBERT

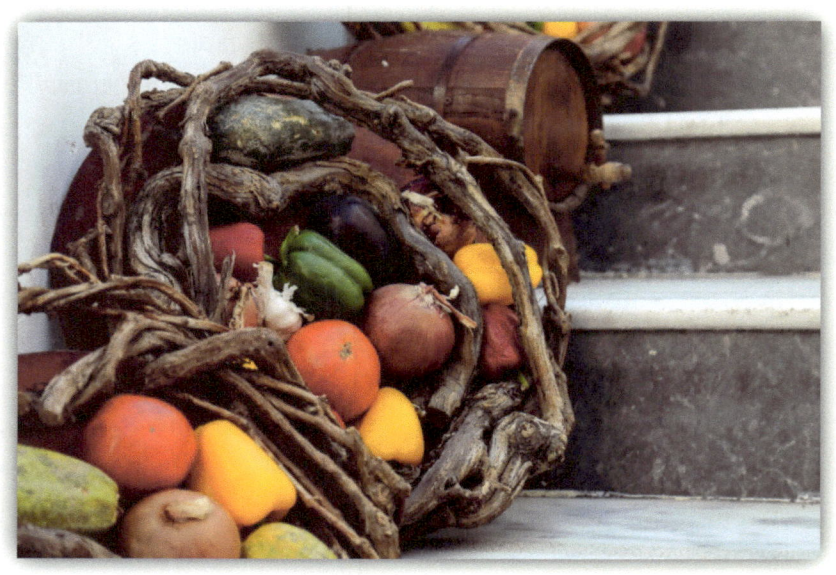

Chapter 1 – 4 Key Things That Make a Picture "Money Worthy" – Regardless of Where You Sell It

When it comes to selling pictures, you can sell a picture of almost any subject (we'll talk about that in later chapters!), but there are a few key things about the picture itself, <u>regardless</u> of subject, that make all the difference as far as sale-ability. If you think about these things, when choosing equipment, when taking photos, and when deciding which photos you plan to sell, you will find that sales will be easier to make, and that your average return on sales will be better. And, most likely, your reputation as a skilled photographer, whose work is a desirable commodity, will grow faster!

Make sure that you have read the instruction book for your camera, and can find the sort of information that I talk about below – most modern cameras have more features than anyone expects, and learning all the detail about yours will help your photography immensely.

So – What are those things ? They are:

1. **Photographic quality**
2. **Framing**
3. **Feel**
4. **Good 'Post-processing'**

Let's look at each of those in a bit more detail:

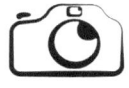

1. Photographic quality :

For Photos to be saleable they need to be of a fairly high photographic quality – that doesn't mean that you need to spend huge amounts on a camera, but is does mean that you need to carefully consider the capability of the camera you choose. Size of camera is not as much of an indicator as it used to be – technology can pack amazing capability into small packages !

So, when choosing a camera, you will need to consider the mega pixel count (that's the number of pixels, or dots of information, that the camera's sensor can capture) that it is capable of – anything less than about 10 Megapixel will not give you enough detail in your photos to sell them in some places.

Here are some examples. This is the same picture, from the same camera, where the only thing different is the number of pixels / dots per inch that the image is saved at. Each image is saved at exactly the same dimensions (10 cm x 7 cm (4 x 3 inches) if you printed it full size). The only difference is the number of dots per inch, in that size, available for the picture to be 'drawn with'. As you can see, the one with 72 dots per inch is much less sharp and detailed than the others. Most sites will want a minimum of 300dpi – that means your camera must be able to take pictures with enough detail, out of the camera, to support that.

The Photographer's Quick Guide to Earning Money From Your Photos

72 dpi

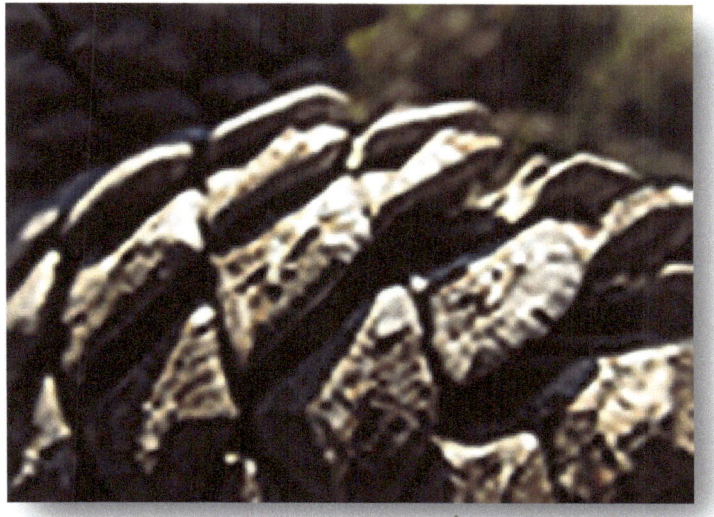

150 dpi

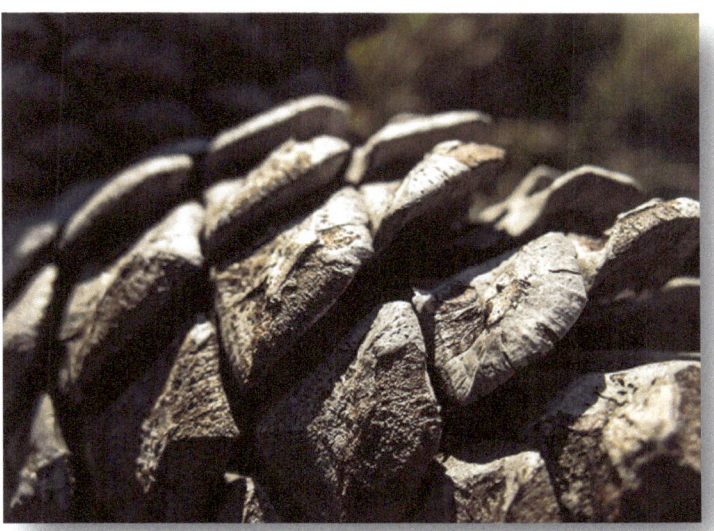

KIM LAMBERT

300 dpi

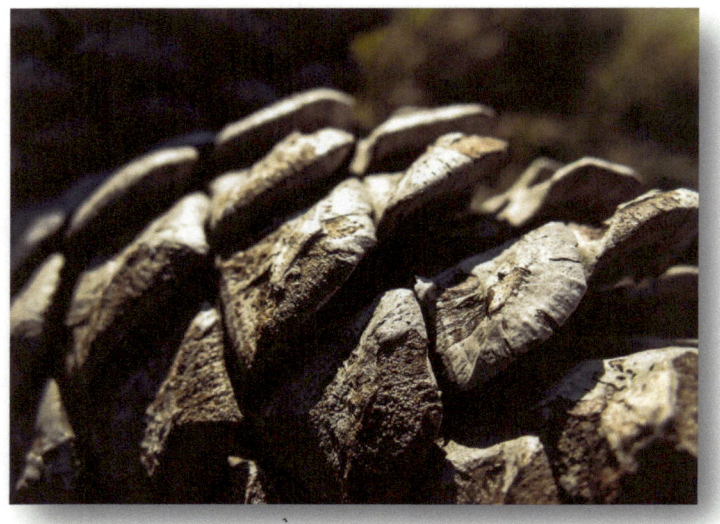

600 dpi

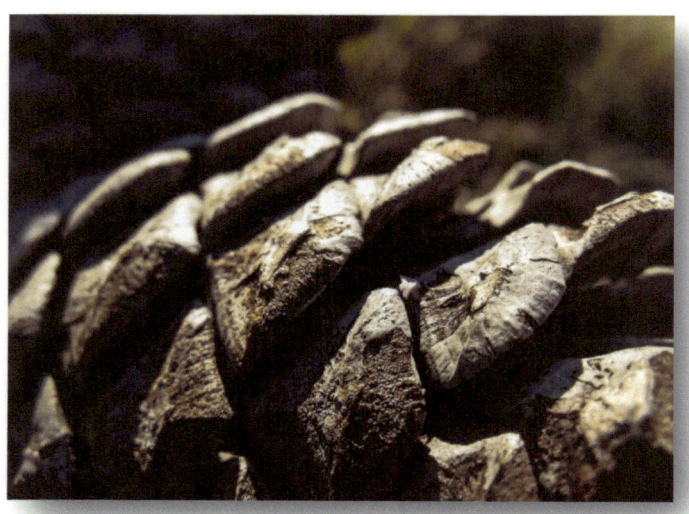

The Photographer's Quick Guide to Earning Money From Your Photos

You will also need to consider sharpness of focus – that is a combination of the camera's capability, especially its lens (whether that is integral or interchangeable, the optical quality matters), and your ability to focus the camera (or convince its autofocus to focus) on exactly where in your picture you want the main focus to be, as well as your ability to hold still. Wobbly people means blurry pictures! (although many cameras today have 'image stabilization' capability, which certainly helps).

Lighting is also a critical part of photographic quality – and whilst that is influenced, obviously, by the amount of natural, or artificial, light present when you take the photo, it is also influenced by the light capability of the camera – the higher 'ISO' that the camera is able to do, the less light you will need in the environment to get the same quality of picture (so you can take good pictures, in darker conditions, even without a flash).

The final key element of photographic quality is color quality – have you ever looked at an item on Ebay, or on an online sale site, and the color of the picture has looked completely different from the color stated in the description? Achieving good color quality comes from being aware of the camera's capability in the aspects already described here, and really looking at the results you are getting, when you review your picture just after you take it.

If you have any doubts, adjust the lighting, or your camera settings, and take another shot. Small variations can be adjusting in post processing (see point 4 below) but the better the original, the higher the end quality will be.

Here is an example – in the first shot, the focus is on the wrong part of the plant – the key feature is blurred.

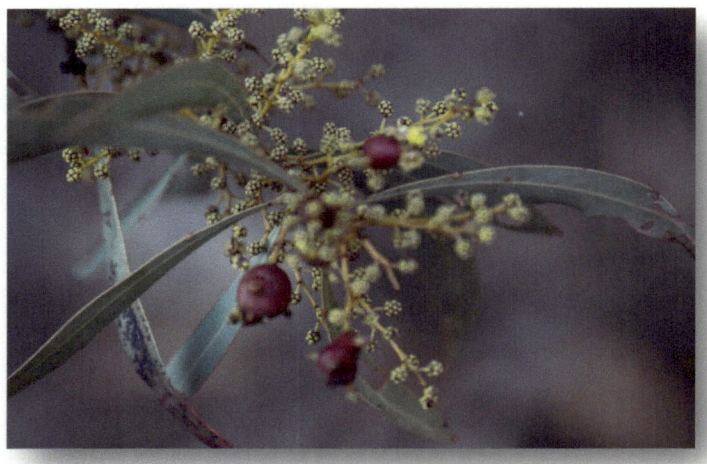

Whereas in the second shot, the key feature of the plant is the part that is in best focus.

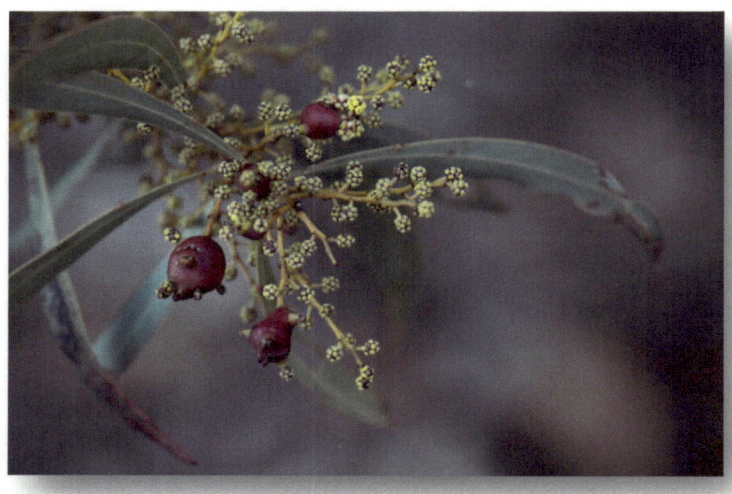

The Photographer's Quick Guide to Earning Money From Your Photos

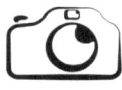

2.   Framing :

How you 'frame' your shot makes all the difference between a very marketable picture, and an amateur 'snapshot'. You will need to think about what is visible in the background, and whether the angle you are shooting from will do strange things to how the perspective looks. Look for different ways to see things – taking a picture of the same thing from down low, will make it look bigger and very different from taking a picture up high.

Also consider how close you need to get – will it look better if you have just the main subject in the shot, with very little background, or does the background add context, or scale, that makes it look better ? Try for very clean backgrounds (unless the background is intentionally busy for context) – something taken against a plain background will stand out better, and jump out of the shot more dramatically when viewed, than something surrounded by lots of 'visual clutter'.

Don't always put the main subject of your picture in the centre! Think about how it will look if you put it off to one side, or towards top or bottom – things often look much more dramatic if they are offset (and if you intend to sell your photo as stock, people who use it to make, for example, and advertising picture, will want some space to put text on top of it...).

A good rule is to imagine a grid of nine squares on your picture, and make the most interesting part of the picture NOT the central square.

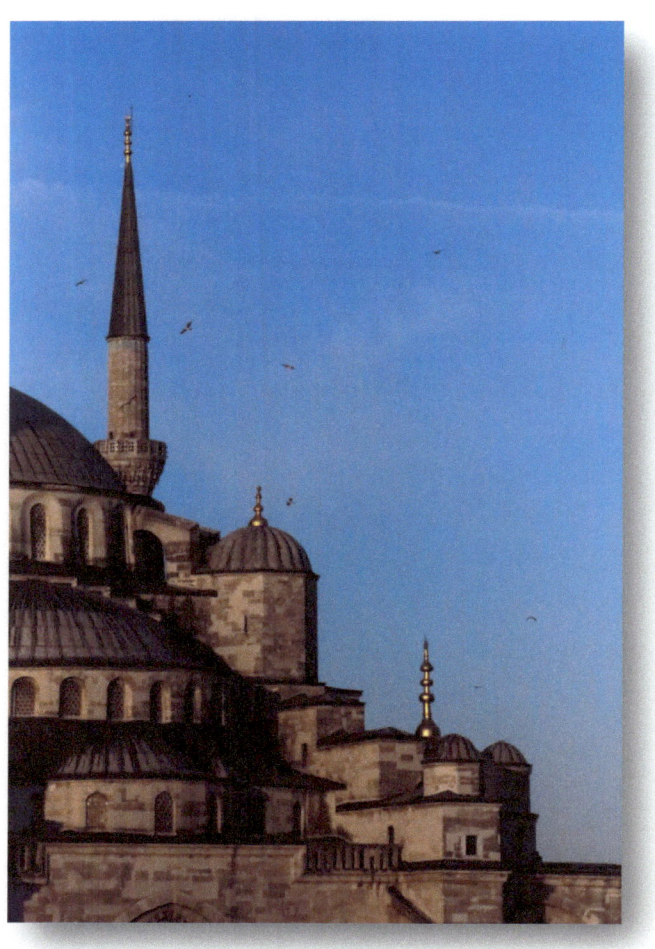

This shot of part of a church in Istanbul is much more dramatic for not being centered – it gives a much stronger impression of the size of the building.

The Photographer's Quick Guide to Earning Money From Your Photos

Here are two shots of the same white rose – one centered, and one a bit offset.

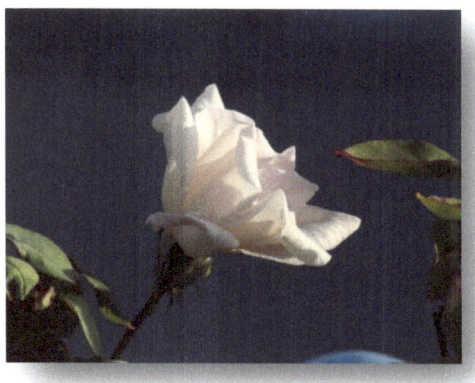

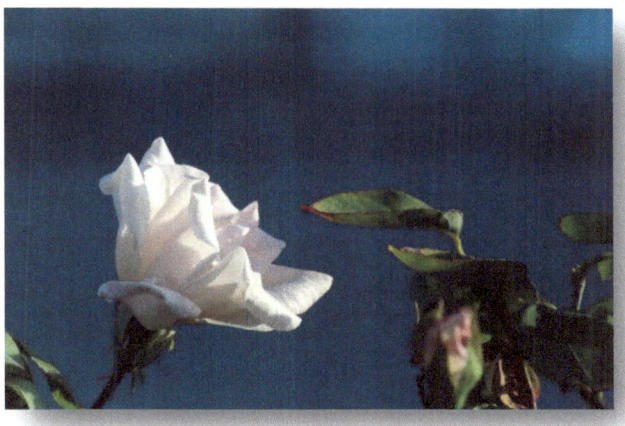

The offset one draws the eye more to the center of the frame, as both the rose and the leaves 'look' to the middle – the overall effect is more pleasing. It's a small change, with a huge effect.

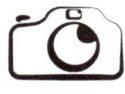

3. Feel :

People buy pictures because they evoke a feeling in them. Like most things, people buy something to make themselves feel good. So, whether someone is buying a big print of your photo, to hang on their lounge room wall, or a graphic artist is buying it to use in constructing an advertisement or a website design, they want something that immediately captures the 'feel' that they want to experience, or that they want to create for another viewer of the result.

If its winter, and there is snow outside, and you look at a picture of a tropical beach, or someone lying beside a stunning blue pool, how do you feel ?

That immediate rush of "wish I was there" emotion, often accompanied by the memory of the feel of sand, or the smell of tropical fruit is the kind of thing that you want your pictures to convey. So when you take a picture, think about "what is the emotion in this scene /item?" "What feeling do I want to capture ?", "What is the essence of the idea I want to capture ?".

Pictures that capture 'feel' or 'emotion' well, outsell technically better pictures every time!

The Photographer's Quick Guide to Earning Money From Your Photos

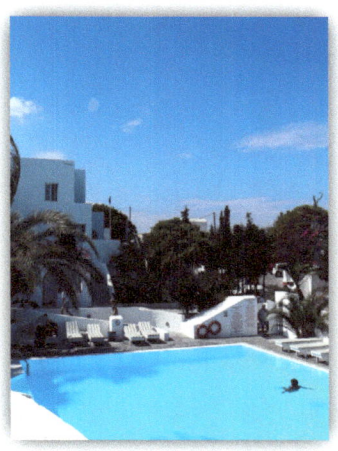

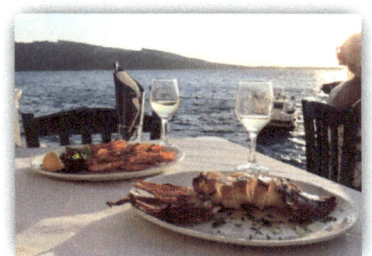

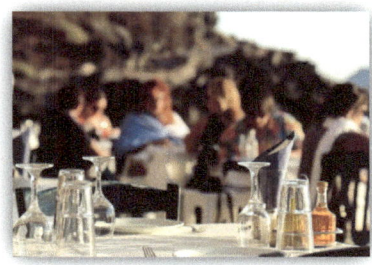

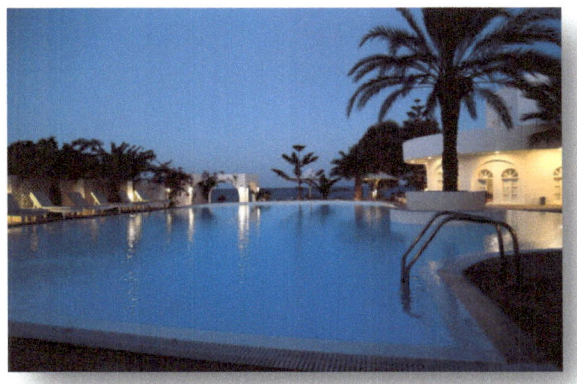

So.... Does this make you feel like a holiday in the Greek Islands would be good ?

KIM LAMBERT

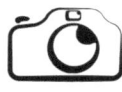

4.   Good Post-Processing :

"What's Post-Processing ?" I can hear many of you ask. It is, without question, one of the major benefits of the digital era of photography.

'Post-Processing' is a catch all term for adjustments that you do to your picture, after you've taken it and transferred it from your camera to your computer. On your computer, using clever software specifically designed for photographers (like Adobe Lightroom), or for graphic designers (like Adobe Photoshop) you can adjust and correct all sorts of things, like the 'white balance' (picture too 'yellow looking'? no problems, let's just change that!), or cropping out an annoying light pole that is just in the edge of the shot etc, etc.

You can, and should, fix the little things, every time.

You can also do things like get rid of 'artifacts' from where there was a speck of dust on your lens, or you can increase how 'romantic' a portrait or a picture of a rose, looks, by creating a 'vignette' effect – a soft paled/blurred out around the edges look, that forces the eye away from, and covers up, any annoying things in the background, and makes you just look at the subject.

The scope is almost endless, and it allows the photographer to be a creative artist across a wide range of ideas, really fast.

The Photographer's Quick Guide to Earning Money From Your Photos

From this original photo of a rose – pretty ordinary, and not the best exposure: -

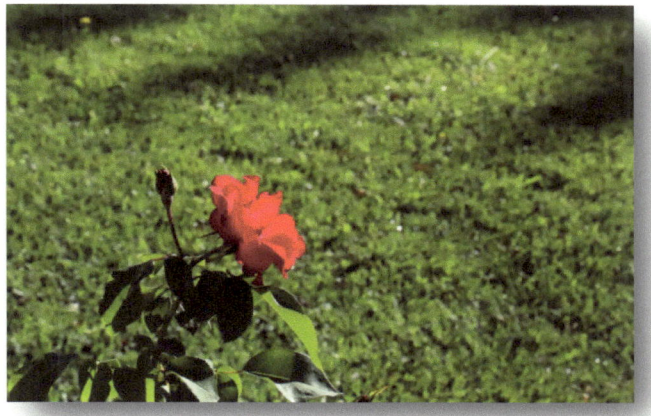

A little post processing can get you to this : - cropped, better color and exposure, and vignetted with a soft blur.

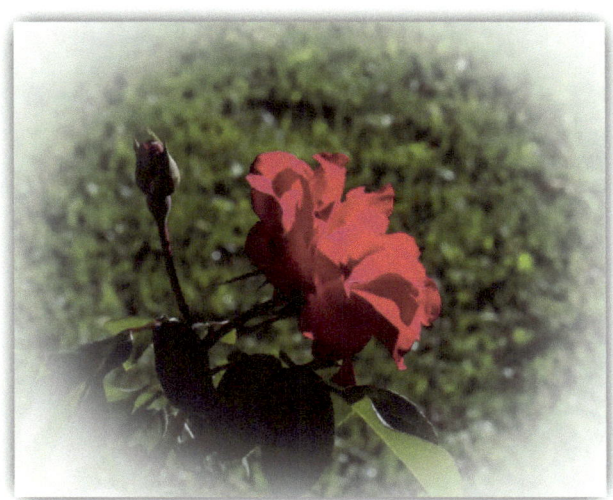

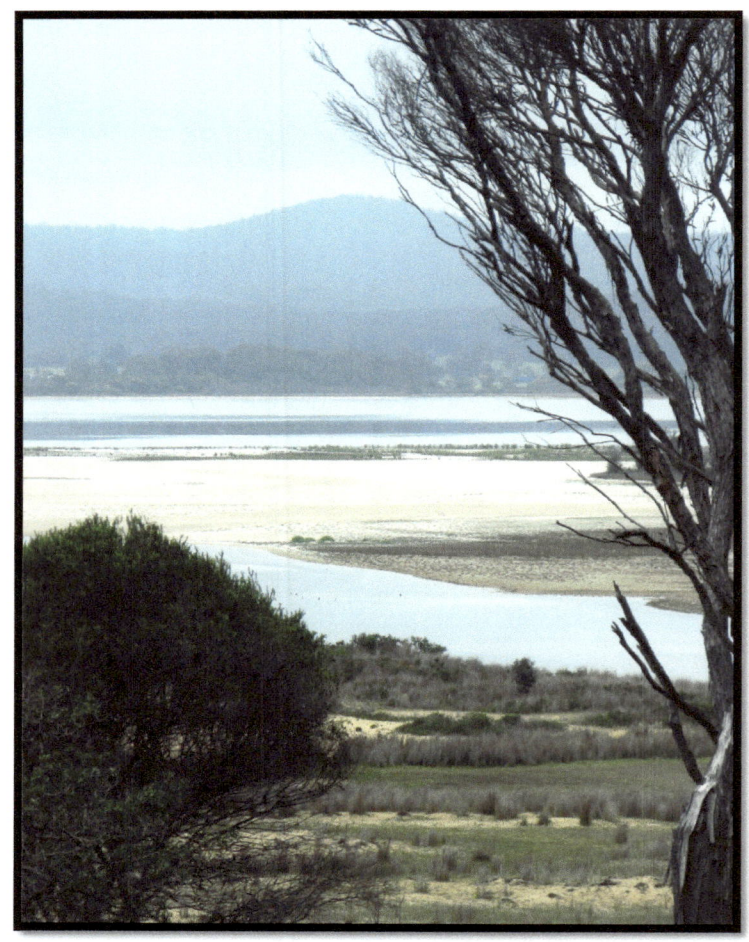

This picture could be sold in a number of ways – as a moody fine art shot for someone to hang on their wall, as a 'capturing the local environment' shot if you live in a coastal area, or as a stock photo shot, especially if it was taken in a national park or named recreation area.

Chapter 2 – 8 Places/Ways You Can Sell Your Photos

There are many places that you can sell your photos, with different amounts of work required on your part, and different sorts of $ returns as a result.

In this chapter we have a look at a few of them, in summary – for more detail on each, please see other books in the series, which focus on those sales channels.

The key thing to realize is that the era of digital photography, high quality home printers, and online shopping has completely changed the options that a photographer has to sell their work.

The more you consciously look for possibilities, the more ways you will find to make your photography pay you (for having fun!).

Here are 8 ideas to get you started!

KIM LAMBERT

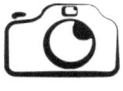

1. Online stock photo sites (see book 12 of this series)

A stock photo site is a place where graphic designers, web site designers, book illustrators or others who need images to use in work that they are creating can go to buy the rights to use a particular image.

Rights granted vary, depending on how much they pay, based on what they want to do with the photo, and what size resolution image they want. The cost of buying a low resolution image can be less than a dollar, if they want to use it in a limited fashion, but the cost of buying a high resolution image, with the intent of using it in a book with a known print run of over 250,000 can run to hundreds of dollars.

When you submit your pictures to a stock photo site, they will assess them, based on their criteria, and if they accept them, your pictures will be available for people to buy through them, and you will be paid a percentage of the sale prices. There are a lot of stock photo sites – some specialize in certain types of photos, others are more general.

They all have different criteria for what they will accept, but the key points in Chapter 1 will put you in a good starting place to get accepted. Most of the sites have a clear explanation of what they will and won't accept, and many have excellent tutorial courses, some with tests to check you've 'got it' about how to make sure your work meets their requirements.

The Photographer's Quick Guide to Earning Money From Your Photos

Even if you never submit to them, these tutorials are an excellent way to learn and improve your photography.

It may take a few tries to get started, but persist, and soon you will have a steady trickle of income rolling in.

If you are interested in learning a lot more about taking photos just for stock photography (even more detail than I cover in book 12 of this series!), and improving your photography skills as you do, you will be interested in the material at the Breakfast Stock Club, on the Photographers Life website, at Http://www.thephotographerslife.com/bsc/kl/

See the Resources Section at Chapter 7 of this book for a list of possible sites – this is not exhaustive, but is a starting point for you.

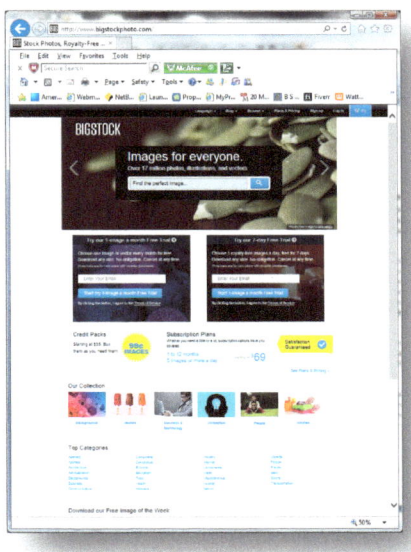

KIM LAMBERT

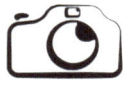

2. Online art and photo sales sites (see book 12 of this series)

Online art and photography sales sites are different from stock photo sites, in that they are aimed at people who want to buy a print to put on their wall, or a picture to use as computer wallpaper, or a calendar with nice pictures, or a T-shirt, iphone cover or other piece of merchandise with unique designs. They are an 'artist's marketplace' and are aimed at a higher price per item and a more exclusive concept.

You create the design, and the site sells, manufactures and ships the item, and pays you a percentage of the sale price.

Different sites have quite different preferred styles, so it's best to have a look at what they promote on their home pages, and at what is most popular and selling (if their site shows you that) before deciding which sites you want to list your work on, so that you can maximize your potential sales. There are lots of creative opportunities here, especially if you like playing about with your pictures in Photoshop or similar, to generate various different effects.

These sites let you create a 'portfolio page' just for you, and that makes it easy to send possible customers to the site, and have them land where the first things they see are just your work. S ee the Resources Section at Chapter 7 of this book for a list of possible sites – this is not exhaustive, but is a starting point for you.

The Photographer's Quick Guide to Earning Money From Your Photos

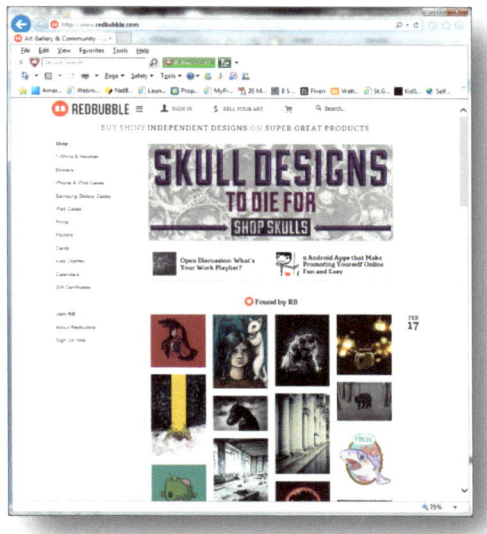

This is Redbubble.com – below is my portfolio there.

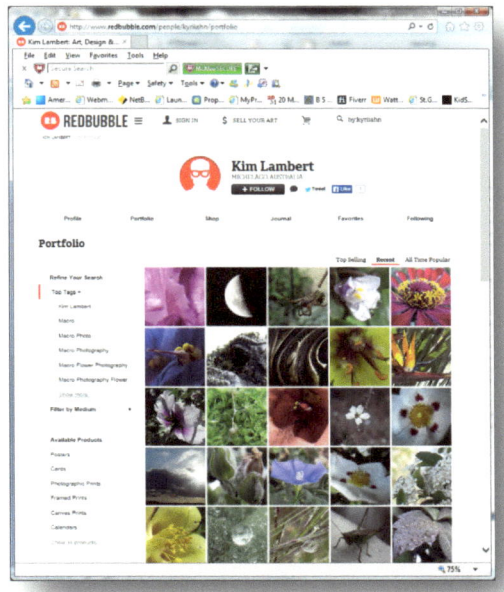

KIM LAMBERT

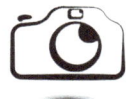

3. **Online T-shirt creation sites (see book 12 of this series)**

Online T shirt creation sites are sites which are primarily aimed at the creation of designs for, and sale of, T-shirts and Hoodies with graphical designs of some kind.

These may be purely for that, or may be a section of a site the also sells other artwork in other formats.

You create the design, and the site sells, manufactures and ships the item, and pays you a percentage of the sale price.

The buying public on these sites is a very different demographic to that on the 'artist's market' style sites. Buyers on a T-shirt specific site may be looking for graphics aimed more around particular sports, or current trending themes, so a bit more research is needed before deciding what you might try to sell through these sites.

See the Resources Section at Chapter 7 of this book for a list of possible sites – this is not exhaustive, but is a starting point for you.

The Photographer's Quick Guide to Earning Money From Your Photos

Here is what Teespring.com looks like

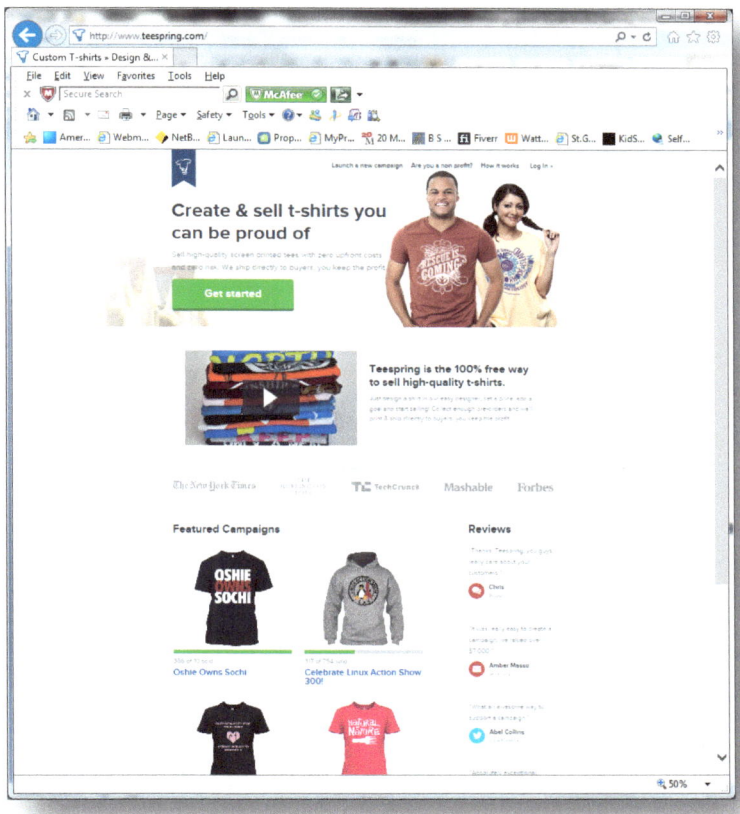

Redbubble (mentioned in the previous point in this chapter) also has a section for selling T-shirts.)

KIM LAMBERT

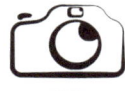

4. **As part of a book (see book 10 of this series)**

Books nearly always have illustrations of some kind, even if it's just the cover. You can sell your pictures to those who create book covers, to those who illustrate books or to publishers of 'local attraction' style 'coffee table books' or magazines.

You can also create your own photo based books to sell, either on specialist book creation sites (who will usually have an integrated books store, through which you can list your book for sale), or on Amazon.com, using their print on demand or Kindle e-book publishing.

If that sounds a bit challenging, there are services who can help you publish, so that all you have to do is create your book, using the template provided, and wait for your payments. These services will charge you a fee to manage the rest for you, but that can be well worth it.

The advantage of doing a series of books is that you can choose topic areas that suit your interests, and the portfolio of pictures that you may already have on hand. With Books, marketing is key – do some research first, and get an idea of whether there is interest in your topic, so that you can maximize your possible sales. See the Resources Section at Chapter 7 of this book for a list of possible sites – this is not exhaustive, but is a starting point for you.

The Photographer's Quick Guide to Earning Money From Your Photos

Here is the front page of Blurb.com, and the sales page for the books that I have on there.

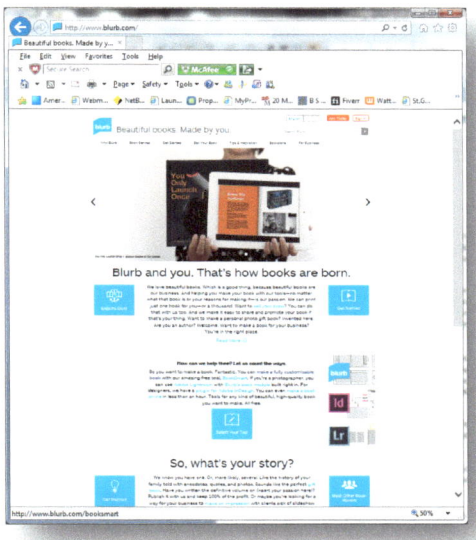

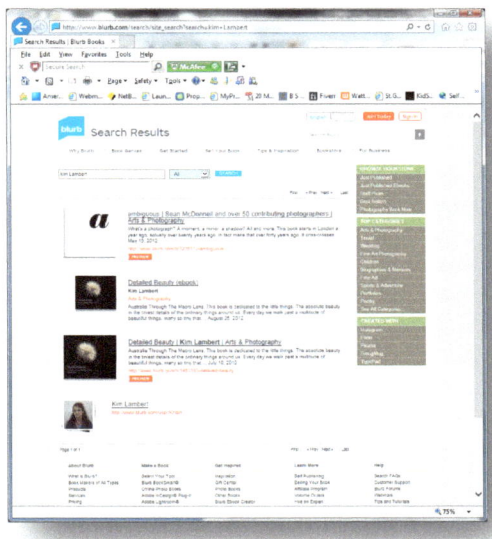

And here is the front page of Createspace, and what one of my books, published through Createspace, looks like when listed on Amazon.com

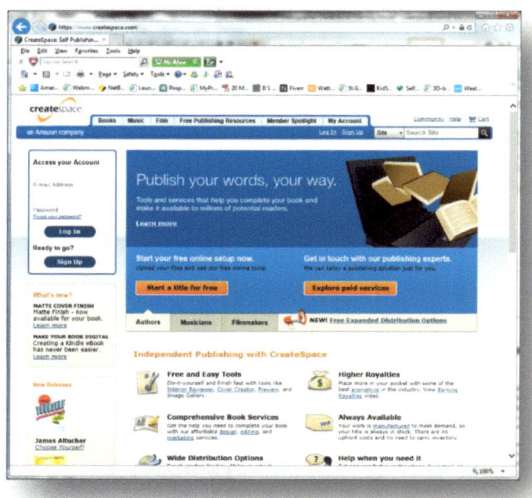

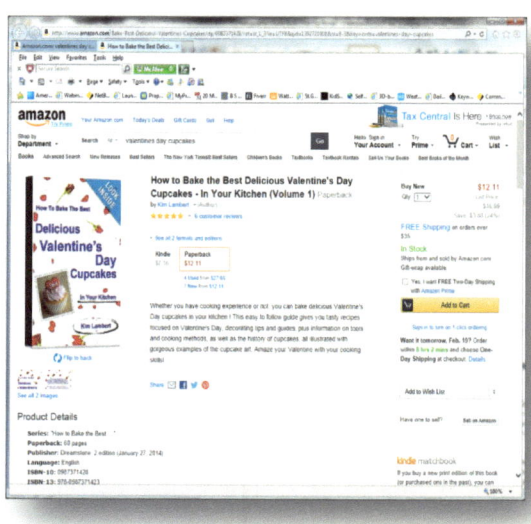

The Photographer's Quick Guide to Earning Money From Your Photos

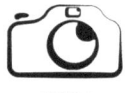

5. In a local coffee shop or restaurant (see book 11 of this series)

Many coffee shops and restaurants want to have some variety in their interior décor – and the easiest way to do that, is to have the pictures on the wall change regularly.

Such places have a large volume of people go through them every day, and while waiting for their food and drink, or sitting and enjoying it, most people will look around them and consider the pictures that they see.

Rather than a coffee shop or restaurant continually spend money on buying pictures to decorate their walls, most are very open to the concept of putting YOUR pictures on their wall, with a price tag, and collecting a percentage of the sale price when one sells.

They make money rather than spending it, and you make money, while their clients get ever changing interesting décor – it's a win-win-win!

If you live in a tourist centric town, or somewhere with iconic scenery, then try to aim for a place where the tourists go, and pictures that capture the 'essence' of the local scenery and character.

You will, to take advantage of this opportunity, have to put out some money up front to get nice prints of your work, and put them in good looking frames, but, when a small print can sell for $200 and up off a coffee shop wall, that is not such a difficult thing, once you have the first few done.

Start by doing some research – look into all of the coffee shops and restaurants in your area, and see which ones have enough wall to be suitable, and may be interested, then get a couple of prints framed, and, taking them with you as a sample, go talk to the shop owners and ask if they will give it a try.

If your local coffee shop is very 'coffee aficionado' focused, then something like this will most likely appeal to them.

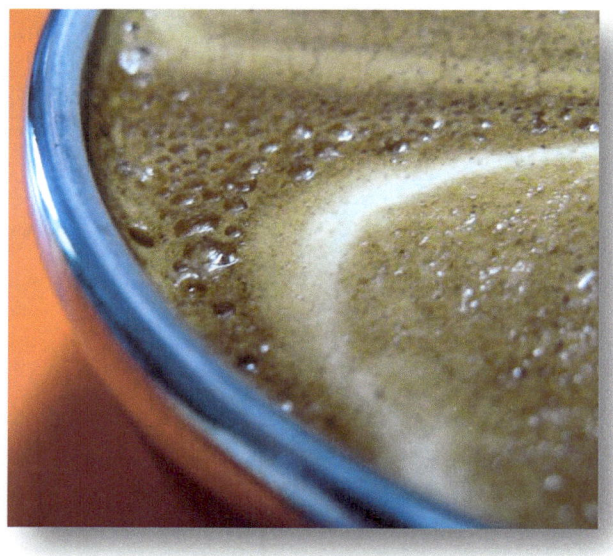

The Photographer's Quick Guide to Earning Money From Your Photos

If you live in, or near, a beach town, this sort of thing is likely to be popular, anywhere that visitors to the town are likely to go.

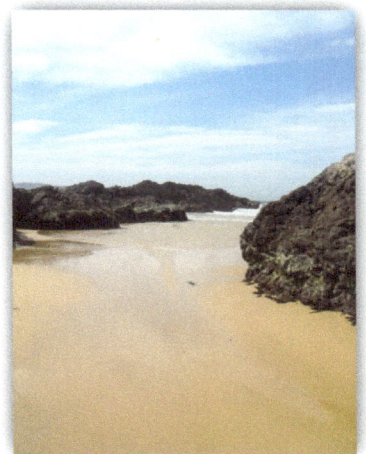
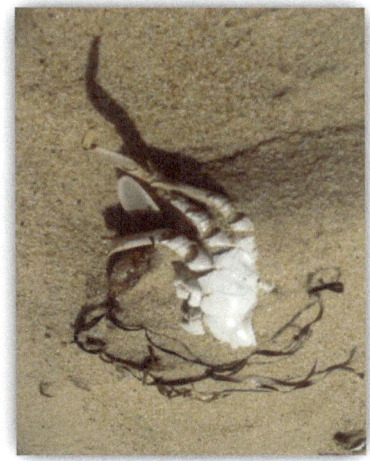
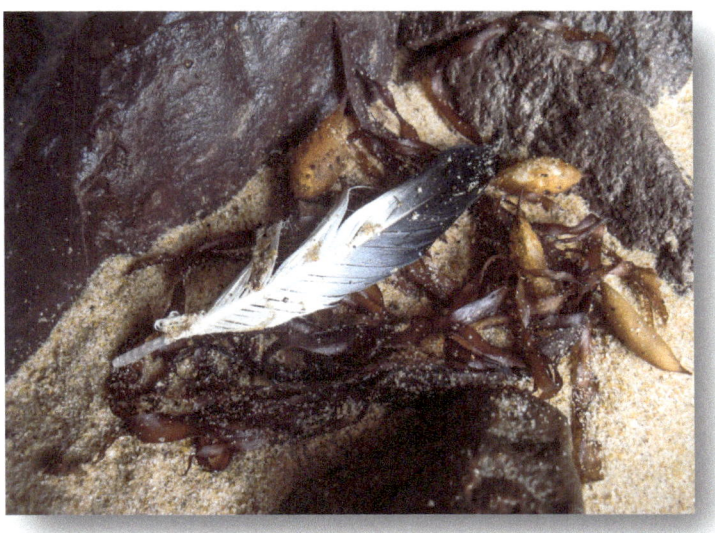

KIM LAMBERT

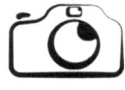

6. In a gallery (see book 11 of this series)

Galleries, in most people's thoughts, are all about paintings, or maybe sculpture. The reality is though, that many galleries do exhibitions of all kinds of art, including photography.

There are two kinds of gallery – ones which arrange all of their own exhibitions, and often focus narrowly on a specific type of art, and those that hire their gallery space to anyone whose material fits their general criteria, and who is willing to pay the space rental, and a percentage of sales to the gallery owner. The former more often host high priced exhibitions from very well known artists, the latter tend to focus more on those just starting out, who have quality work to show.

Don't think that you need lots and lots of printed and framed pieces of work to do an exhibition – this is a space where less is more! Depending on the size of the gallery space, between 10 and 40 pieces will be more than enough.

You will need to arrange the prints and framing yourself, but the gallery owner may be able to advise and assist with getting that done.

Ask around – you will be surprised how many gallery spaces may be available in your area.

The Photographer's Quick Guide to Earning Money From Your Photos

You will need to decide if you are going to make the pieces:

- exclusive - ie, this is the only print of this that will ever be done, outside the photographers personal collection, and the picture will not be licensed for use anywhere else, ever – in which case the buyer gets to collect the piece the day after the exhibit closes.

- or semi exclusive - ie, there will only ever be 10 signed numbered prints of this picture – in which case buyers pay and order while it is on display and you deliver to all at a nominated point in time after the exhibit.

- or non exclusive – no guarantees that you won't sell another print of the same picture tomorrow.

Generally, the more exclusive you make it, the higher a price you can ask for each piece. BUT…. Your work will need to be of a quality that people will be happy to pay high prices for, with print and framing quality to match, if you do want to go exclusive.

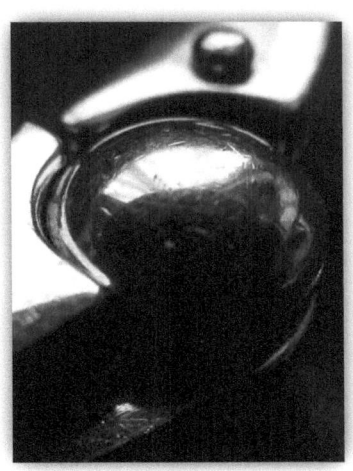

KIM LAMBERT

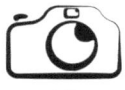

7. **By doing exclusive photo shoots of a targeted type (eg, pets, babies etc) (see book 11 of this series)**

This works best if your specific targeted area is something that you really, _really_ care about yourself. So – if you love dogs, and are into dog training, you could start by offering a 'dog portrait' service to members of your local dog training club. The key is to know enough about the topic to be in a good position to understand what sort of photo will make your clients feel like you have really captured the 'essence' of the subject.

Consider your chosen area carefully, practice, practice, practice, until you are comfortable that you can do the subject/s justice, then look for your best local groups to market your services to. That could be a pet related group, like the example above, or it could be the local mothers club if you like photographing babies, or the local jewelry making club if you like taking macro 'portraits' of beautiful objects.

If you like taking portraits of people, start with your friends, family and neighbors.

Try to capture really nice portraits of them, get them printed and framed, and give them to the subjects, as presents – if you have done it well, they will display your work with pride, others will ask who took the photos, and word of mouth will do your marketing for you.

The Photographer's Quick Guide to Earning Money From Your Photos

Trying to be "a professional photographer" in the traditional sense, and setting up a business that tries to take good pictures of anything and everything is setting yourself up to fail – get specialized, and let your expertise in that one area make you shine.

Always look for unusual or different angles on your topic area too. If your picture looks 'just like' many others in the topic area, no-one will notice – you need to capture things in a way that stands out, that makes people look, and look again.

Here is an example of making a portrait very different from the 'standard approach'.

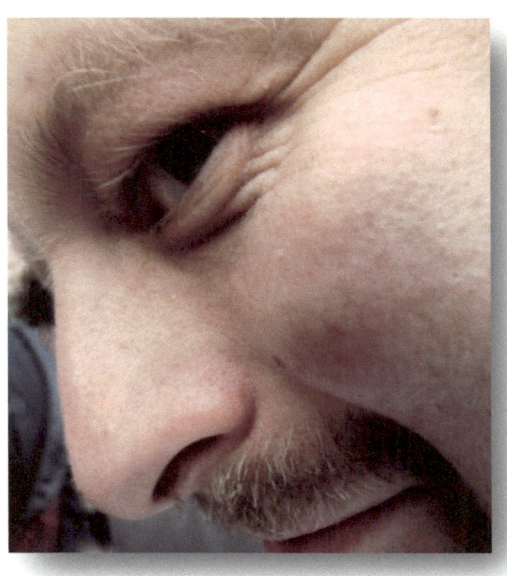

KIM LAMBERT

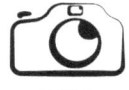

8. **Using your photos to create unique craft items, or selling prints to those who do (decoupage, 'distressed' look mounted prints, scrapbooking, vision-boards) (see book 11 of this series)**

Many people create craft items that are very visually based. Over the last decade there has been an upswell of interest in such activities as scrapbooking – creating books of collated, collected items, pictures and words to make a lasting reminder of places, people or times in your life.

If you live in a resort town, there is almost certainly a market for pictures that are materials for people to use to remember that they have visited.

These don't need to be big prints, just ones that are very representative of your town. Sell through local craft shops, or at markets.

If you find people who like making things with decoupage (where a picture is transferred to the surface of a jewelry box, or other item) they are also likely to be interested in photos that create the feel that they want.

Investigate local craft classes and clubs to find possible clients.

The Photographer's Quick Guide to Earning Money From Your Photos

You can also make items yourself – a particularly successful item in this sort of category is pictures for hanging on people's walls, made by attaching prints of your photos to old boards and carefully creating an aged 'distressed' look.

Choose a picture that captures something that could be 'anywhen', as people who want 'distressed look' style furniture and items are often creating the feel of a particular period in their home.

You can sell this sort of work at markets, through local craft shops, local coffee shops and similar. You can also sell some of this type of work online, through sites like Etsy, or even Ebay.

The same sort of effect can be created by finding old picture frames in thrift shops, and doing some post processing on your photos to create a sepia toned look, or a black and white look, so that the picture and the frame seem to be from a bygone era.

It can be lots of fun to go seeking out locations in your town and surrounds that look 'just like they did 50 years ago', if you catch them at the right time (with no modern cars in the shot!) or from the right angle.

On the next page you can see how that would work, with an example of making something look like an old sepia tone photo.

Here is a shot that I took of a refitted sailing ship which does tours in the caldera at Santorini. First in normal color, second after I made it a sepia look. Imagine the sepia one in an old style frame.

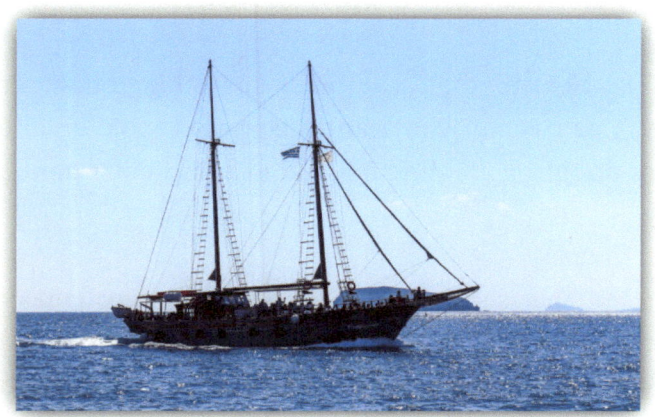

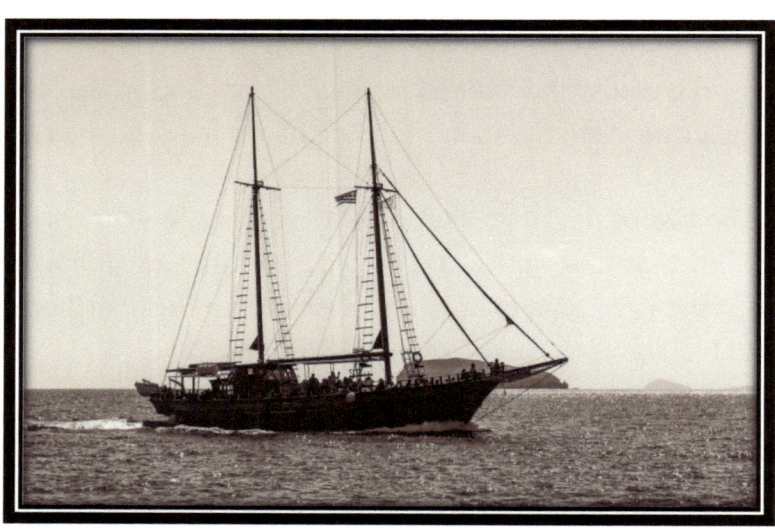

Chapter 3 – 9 Common Mistakes That Can Stop You From Making Money With Your Photos

It is often the small things that make or break the 'money worthiness' of a picture. Here are some of the common mistakes that can cost you money!

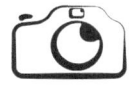

1. Rushing

It seems like it is always the times that we are in a hurry that we see things that will make the best shot. At times like that, it is very tempting to just 'point and click', hope it turns out, and 'keep on rushin'. Then, when we look at the pictures later, we are so disappointed ! Making a habit of NOT rushing can greatly increase the number of 'money worthy' photos that you take. Think about the shot carefully, consider the framing, lighting, background etc, and what you really want from the shot, then take it – and take a few pictures, not just one.

That said, don't be paralyzed by trying to make it perfect – there are times when we have to just push the button, and keep on doing so, in the hope that we will capture the moment before its gone. However, if you do have the time to pause and consider, **<u>do it</u>** !

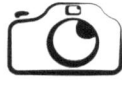

2. Not considering the background (plants out of heads etc)

For as long as there has been photography people have had this simple problem – when we look at something, we focus on the important thing in our view, and our brain edits out the unimportant (which is usually in the background). Unfortunately for us, the camera does not make judgments about what is important – it just faithfully captures absolutely everything in its view.

So – it is very easy to take a picture that is perfect in every way, except for that potted plant in the background, that happens to look like its growing out of Uncle John's head......

These days, we have Photoshop and similar, and if we are good at post processing we *may* be able to edit it out, but we may not.

The Photographer's Quick Guide to Earning Money From Your Photos

It is infinitely better to simply not have the potted plant in the picture to begin with! So be aware of the background – really look at it, and consider what the camera will see. Then choose a different spot, a different angle, move things that you don't want in the picture – whatever it takes to get it right to start with, rather than have to try to fix it later, in the computer.

Here is an example of a bad background moment – this shot of a delicious plate of food on a table with wine has a very unfortunate lamp post appearing to rise straight out of the wine carafe. In this case, there was no available angle when I took this where I could get a better background, So the second picture shows the same shot, after I edited the lamppost out of the picture using Photoshop

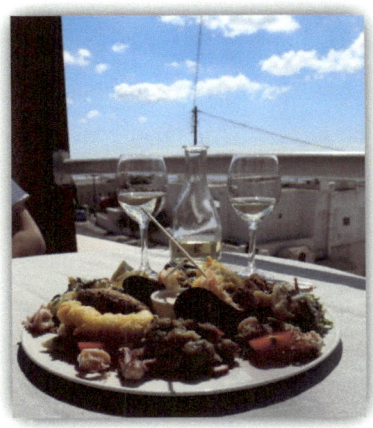 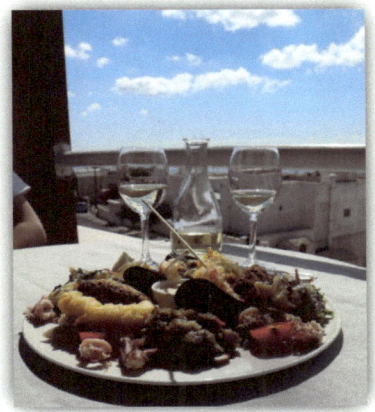

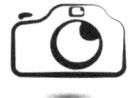

3. Using too cheap a camera

Whilst the quality available for the money in cameras today is truly amazing, there are still some distinct limitations. If you want to sell your photos through most stock photo sites, you will have to have a camera that is capable of capturing a large enough quality image to start with.

The Megapixel count of the camera should be as high as you can afford. The optical quality should be as good as you can afford – high megapixel count with a terrible lens is still a terrible picture (in fact, you can see the bad things in more detail!). If you want to be able to zoom in on things, and you are using an integrated lens camera, then the **optical** zoom amount should be as high as possible – digital zoom will give you a grainier, fuzzier result.

An interchangeable lens camera will give you the best result – do some research, and choose the best camera that you can afford, or choose the best place to sell your photos where the camera you have will not put you at a disadvantage. You can now submit photos taken with a mobile phone to some stock sites, so long as the meet certain requirements !

So there is a place for almost any photo to make money, so long as it meets the needs and requirements of that particular use.

The Photographer's Quick Guide to Earning Money From Your Photos

Here are three pictures of the same subject, taken from the same distance away, then cropped to a similar part of the picture (which, for the higher quality camera is a much smaller part of the original frame, even though the end result is still higher quality.

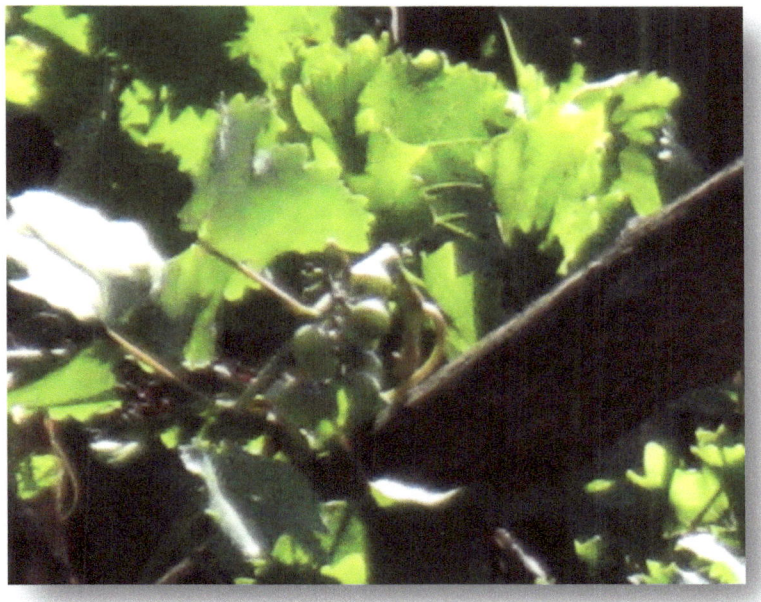

Picture 1 – Canon A720IS (that's a little point and shoot camera, with 6 x optical and 10 x digital zoom), at Full digital zoom 1/800th sec, ISO 400, f4.8 – you can see that its not very sharp or clear

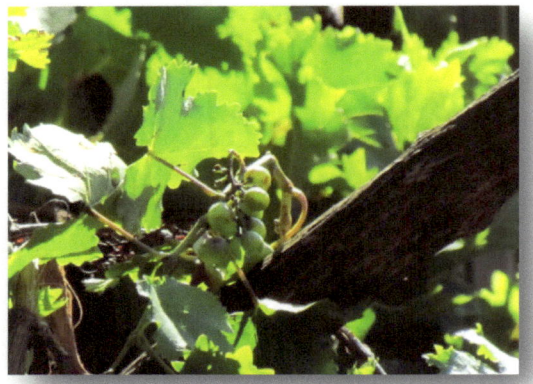

The second picture is from a Canon SX30IS (a higher end point and shoot style camera, but not interchangeable lenses, with 35 x Optical zoom and 6 x digital zoom on top of that) at maximum optical zoom, but no digital zoom, at $1/500^{th}$, ISO-400, f5.8 – you can see that the picture is a lot sharper and clearer.

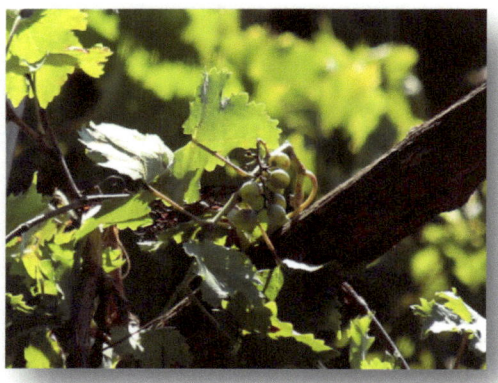

The third picture is from a Canon EOS 6D (a 'pro-sumer' level interchangeable lens camera) using a 70 to 300 mm lens, at 300 mm – so full zoom, all optical, obviously, $1/250^{th}$, ISO 160, f5.6 – you can see that it is much clearer and sharper than either of the others, even though this is a small part of the actual frame.

The Photographer's Quick Guide to Earning Money From Your Photos

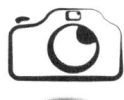

4. Not considering lighting

Lighting is another situation where the human brain does some 'helpful' editing in our daily life.

When we are out in bright light, whilst we will be aware of shadows being cast, we will not pay much attention – if we look at an item that has a 'shadow line' falling across it, we will still understand the object as a whole, and adjust mentally for the light difference.

If we take a photo of that item, we will see a sharp 'shadow line' across the middle of the picture, and either the bright side will be way too bright, or the shadow side will be so dark that there is no detail, or both.

Ideally, for a good photo, lighting should be fairly strong, but very even – so days with a cloudy sky can provide excellent light, as can early or late in the day, when the sun is not so strong (although its angle can be a challenge then).

If you can arrange to have the setup time, using very carefully placed additional lighting can be good, or using a light reflector to reflect more even light back onto the subject can make a huge difference.

This shot of a shell suffers badly from 'photographer's shadow' which the mind has edited out completely when taking the shot.

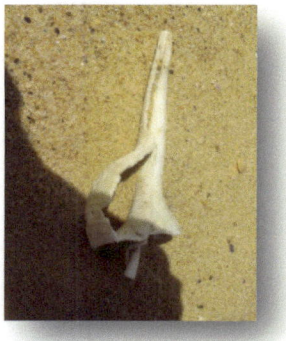

Here are two shots of an alleyway of shops in Istanbul. This sort of scene makes for great photos, but the strong shadow line down the middle of the street detracts from the picture.

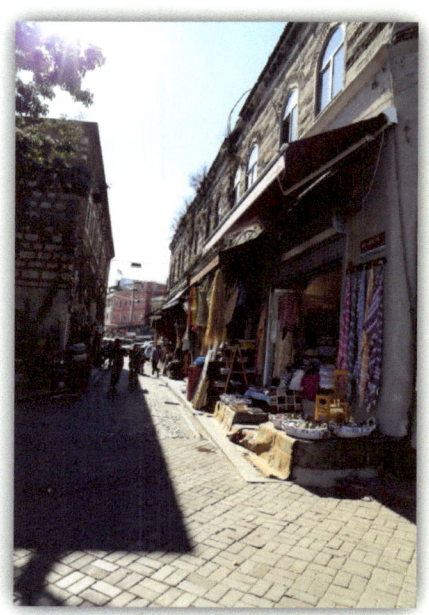

The Photographer's Quick Guide to Earning Money From Your Photos

And here is what the shot looks like after I have adjusted it in Lightroom – better perspective, softer shadows and stronger focus on the bright wares for sale.

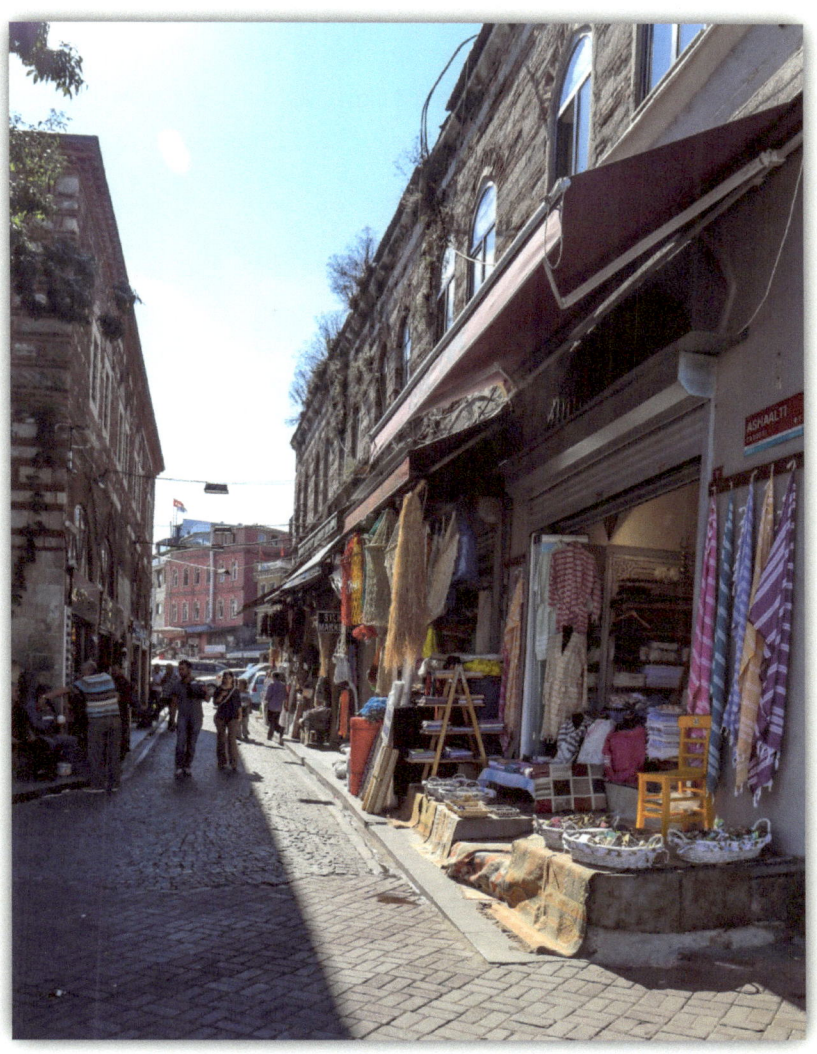

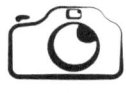

5. Not considering perspective and other angles

Perspective is another interesting area – again, the human brain does some adjusting for us, but taking a picture from the wrong point can produce a result rather like looking into a distorting mirror.

There is an effect called foreshortening – that is what happens when you take a picture of a whole person, standing, from fairly close to them, and it comes out with their head looking huge and their feet looking tiny.

That happens because you were standing up when you took it – if you crouch down so that the camera is at about their waist level, they will come out looking normal, as the perspective will be correct for the camera.

Position is critical to getting a good photo that is both interesting, and really captures your subject. This is why you often see photographers on their knees, or in odd positions – they are trying to get the best angle on a shot, to ensure that they get a 'money worthy' picture, not just a snapshot.

When you photograph anything, always consider the perspective, and whether it will look better / more interesting / not 'the usual' if you move around and capture it from another angle.

The Photographer's Quick Guide to Earning Money From Your Photos

Here are two examples of taking a different view:

This is the bell tower of a church in Pyrgos, on Santorini – people tend to photograph whole buildings, but taking just this part of it, from the unusual angle, really emphasizes the intensity of the white tower against the blue sky, and gives a sense of how tall it is.

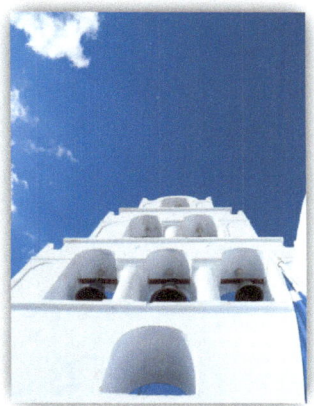

And this is the edge of the baptismal font, in the Basilica in San Jose, with just a few drops of water fallen, just after a person has dipped their fingers to cross themselves.

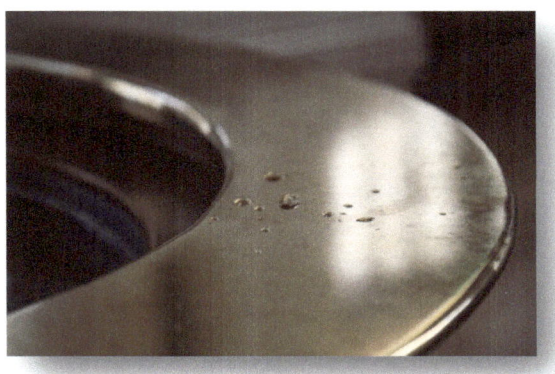

KIM LAMBERT

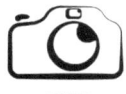

6. Not doing any post processing

Post processing capability is a precious gift of the digital age – USE IT! One reason that almost anyone can earn some money from their photos now, is that you do not have to get it perfect first time (although a certain level of quality is needed).

We now have the luxury of being able to take many shots to (hopefully) make sure that one of them is good, and then of being able to 'tweak' the exposure, white balance, color and framing in post processing.

This should not make you lazy – the best photos are still the ones that are closest to ideal when they come out of the camera – when we have considered everything as we set up and took the shot. But it should make you grateful to have the chance to fix the little things, and be able to use, and sell, pictures that would not be saleable without those fixes.

A classic example is straightening up a horizon. We so often take a picture, concentrating on the foreground, only to discover that the camera was tilted slightly off level, and we have a sloping horizon in the background, not a level one.

With post processing, that's not a problem – we can adjust the angle of the photo, in tiny increments, until its straight, then crop it slightly to make it square again, as if it had been perfect from the start.

The Photographer's Quick Guide to Earning Money From Your Photos

Here is an example:

This is the shot as it came out of the camera – I was so focused on capturing the interesting clouds and pink tones from the sunset, that I was not paying attention to how level I was holding the camera. The exposure is also a bit uneven, with the beach full of empty deck chairs in front too dark

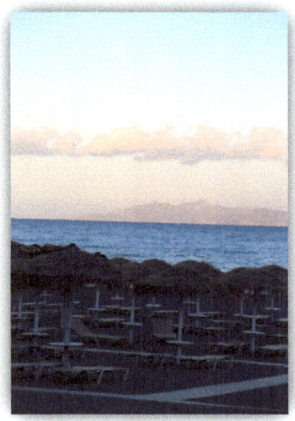

And here it is after some post processing – horizon leveled and exposure adjusted.

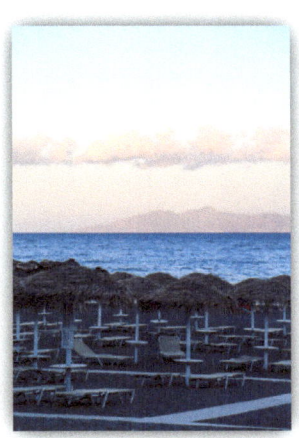

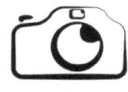

7. Not taking enough shots of the same subject

In the era of film based cameras, the challenge for photographers was to balance cost of film, developing and printing, with the risk of not getting the shot right. Digital cameras have removed that problem for us. Memory cards are cheap, digital cameras let us preview the shot as soon as we have taken it, and we can take it again, and again, until we get it right, so long as the subject stays in place.

So, unless you are photographing something like a bird in flight, where the subject moves so fast that its gone in a few seconds, you have an amazing opportunity. Remember to use it ! The best way to learn what works, is to take dozens of pictures of the same subject, from different angles, with different camera settings, at different levels of close up or far away, and see which ones work best.

You don't even have to note down your settings! The camera records them for you, as metadata which is part of the picture file, and which can be seen as easily as clicking on the picture in Windows file explorer (or equivalent)

Taking lots of shots, and having a few that work really well, is better than agonizing about when to hit the button, and ending up with nothing, because the moment has passed.

The Photographer's Quick Guide to Earning Money From Your Photos

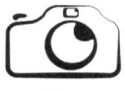

8. Posting too many, and unprotected, photos online (like Flickr and Facebook etc)

These days, everyone posts photos online, right? Well, yes, but if you want to make money from your photos, consider very carefully what you expose, where.

Most photos on Flickr, for example, are automatically listed as under creative commons licensing, which means that someone can download your picture, in various sizes and use it. They are supposed to say that you took it, and where they found it, but people often don't!

Even worse, the conditions of use for sites like Facebook give those sites rights over your pictures that you post there, in a whole range of ways – its worth trawling through the 'legal pages' of the sites to understand what they can do, before you post much.

When you do post pictures in places like that, remember to post them with a digital watermark that states its yours, and at a low resolution, so it's not very useable if someone does decide to download and use it. If you want to post things to advertise your skills, choose pictures that you don't aim to use or sell any other way.

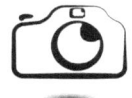

9. Not tracking what you have made available for sale, where

When you submit pictures to stock photo sites, some will want exclusive rights to sell them (and will pay you a higher percentage of each sale as a result).

If you do not implement a system of tracking what pictures you have listed where, you may inadvertently break your contract with them.

Equally, if you sell prints in a gallery, and sell them as single, or limited run exclusive items, you must carefully track how many you have sold of which picture, to ensure that you do not break your advertised guarantee of their exclusivity – after all, exclusivity is what people pay extra for!

So make sure that you track what you do, and keep careful records, from the start.

The easiest way to do this is to use a software product with picture cataloguing capability, preferably one that does lots of other clever post processing things too, like Adobe Lightroom or Rawtherapy and Digikam.

Chapter 4 – 12 Different Kinds of Photography You Can Make Money From

There are many different types of photography – the scope is huge for everyone to find an area of photography that they are interested in, which is also going to allow them to earn money from it.

Traditionally, a photographer who made money from their business, took photos of anything and everything – now that need not be true, and, in many cases, there is a much, much better chance of you making good money by choosing a specific niche and aiming your work at those clients needs and interests.

Here are just a few examples of types of photography that you can concentrate on, if they appeal to you, and earn money with your work. Many of these are covered in more detail in another book in this series, as noted below.

In addition, if you are interested in a detailed, on-line course all about how to Turn Your Pictures into Cash, you will be interested in the information at
http://www.thephotographerslife.com/ph4/kl/

KIM LAMBERT

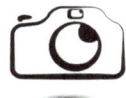

1. **Portraits (see Book 2 in this series)**

Portraits are a core part of the business of many traditional style professional photographers. BUT... you may have noticed that the portraits that you see on peoples walls, taken by the photographic studios that do that sort of thing, are all very similar, even, one could say, rather boring.

So, unless you are taking a picture of someone for them to use in a staid corporate context, where they actually want 'boring', look for ways to be different. Make your portraits stand out, because they do capture the person, as themselves, looking great, looking natural, rather than all posed and stiff. – No gritted teeth smiles in your work! Unusual angles still can capture the essence of a person (or a pet, for that matter!)

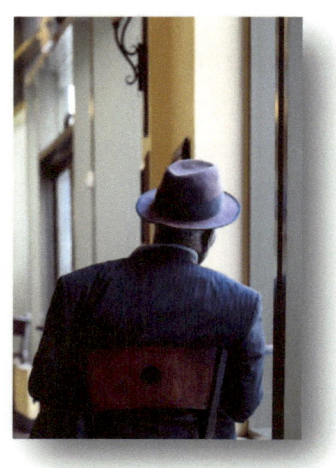

The Photographer's Quick Guide to Earning Money From Your Photos

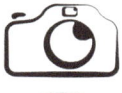

2. Travel Photos (see Book 3 in this series)

A travel photo is intensely about creating a feeling, about making the viewer feel like they are there, wherever in the world 'there' is. Travel photos should make a place look **better** than it does in reality.

Places in travel photos have no litter, no dirt anywhere – they need to look pristine and beautiful – a perfect version of the place, if you want to sell them for advertising, to travel magazines or to create travel books from them. If you are doing a more documentary style, about the contrasts in a place, or the reality of conditions somewhere, then that may be different – but the most saleable travel photos tend to be those that present a place in the best possible light (literally and figuratively!).

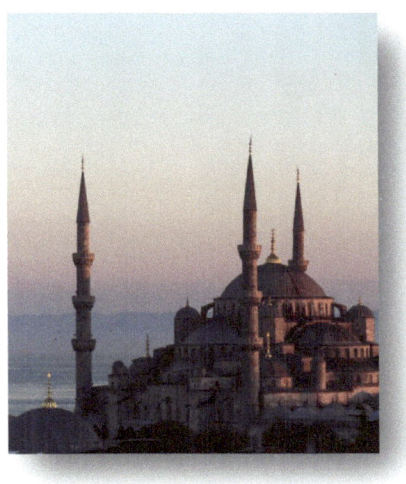

KIM LAMBERT

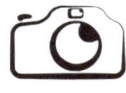

3. Landscapes (see Book 4 in this series)

Landscapes can be a spectacular part of the photographers art – but they can also be one of the most challenging. You have no choice but to work with the natural light, and sometimes may have to wait hours or days to get a shot of a particular piece of scenery with the lighting and weather conditions that you want.

On the other hand there are times when an amazing landscape photo opportunity just presents itself – you may drive around a corner, and there, in front of you, is the perfect shot, with the perfect light.

For landscapes, you need to either set aside planned time, or always carry your camera with you, and be prepared to drop everything and stop to get a shot.

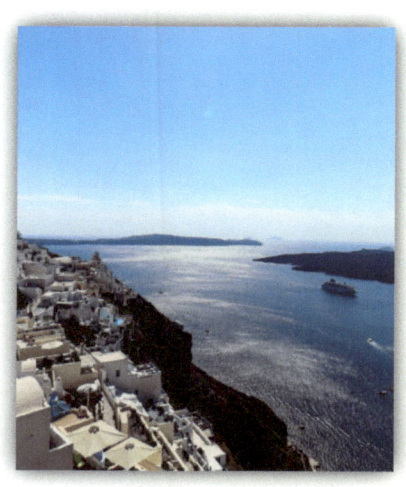

The Photographer's Quick Guide to Earning Money From Your Photos

The difference between a casual snapshot and a stunning landscape picture comes down to framing, as well as lighting. Your local area almost certainly has some beautiful landscape spots, but it is equally likely that they are almost always photographed from the same angle/spot, because that is the easiest place to get a pretty result. Try to find a different angle on those spots!

Seeing a well known landscape feature, from a different angle from the one that is commonly photographed, is an excellent way to create interest (think about iconic landscape shots, like Mt Fuji in Japan – all the shots that you see are from the same vantage point – do you have any idea what it looks like from any other angle ?)

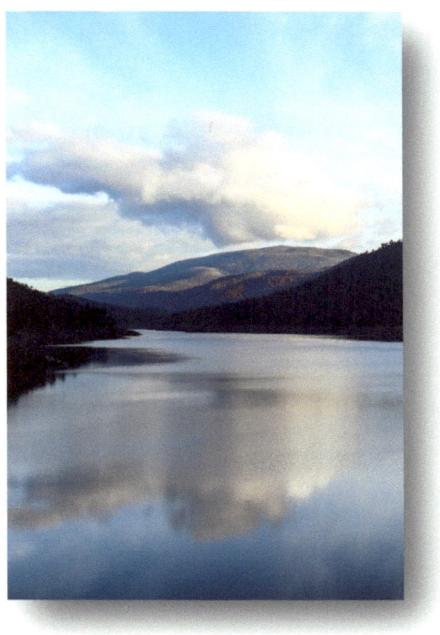

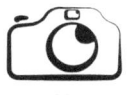

4. Macro (Super Close up) Photos (see Book 5 in this series)

Macro photography (taking super close ups of things, whether that is insects, the details of flowers, a piece of beautiful jewelry, the stitches in an embroidery, or anything else where detail is small and amazing) was long considered a very challenging task, limited to the few who could afford expensive specialist lenses and lighting.

Not so any more. Modern digital cameras, even quite small and basic ones, have a macro setting (that's the one with the icon that looks like this – ❀) which allows you to take photos of things up very, very close, sometimes as close as 1/5 th of an inch (that's ½ a cm), and still have perfect focus, without you needing to know what settings to make.

When you take a macro photo of something, depending on what camera and settings you are using, you will generally find that the depth of field (that's how much of the foreground and background are in focus) is very shallow.

This means that you need to be very careful about where on the subject you want the focus to be, but it also means that you almost effortlessly get that lovely effect where the main subject of the picture is sharp, but the background is out an of focus soft blur of color – so the main subject really stands out against it. That effect is called bokeh.

The Photographer's Quick Guide to Earning Money From Your Photos

Macro photos are often used in advertising, or in creating web page headers or backgrounds, because they provide intense detail with no distracting clutter.

Here is an example of the bokeh effect.

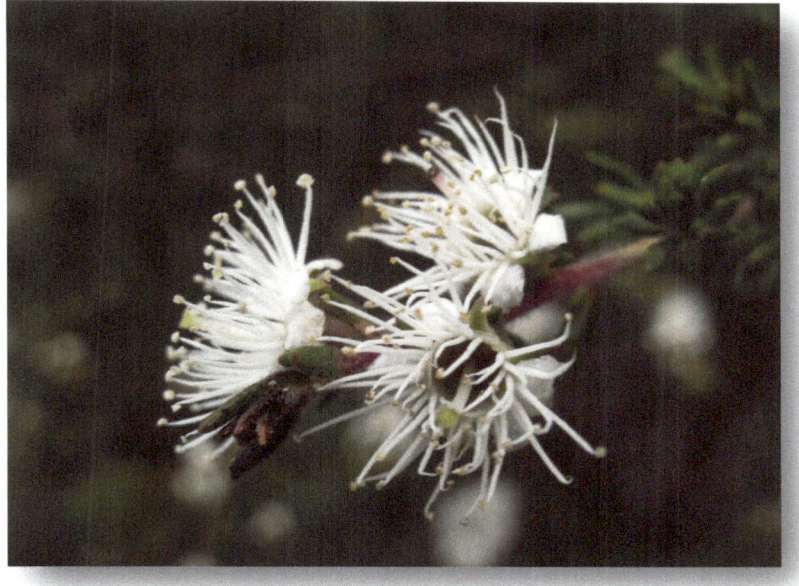

See my book "Detailed Beauty: Australia Through the Macro Lens" for more work like this, at http://www.blurb.com/b/1463183-detailed-beauty

KIM LAMBERT

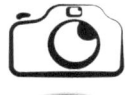

5. Urban and Industrial photography (see Book 6 in this series)

This is an interesting area for a photographer. Most people think of beauty as being most represented by the natural environment, but beauty can equally be found in the shapes and textures of the manmade environment.

Many buildings have amazing shapes and reflective surfaces, and public art pieces, often constructed of metal can create aspects and angles which make amazing pictures.

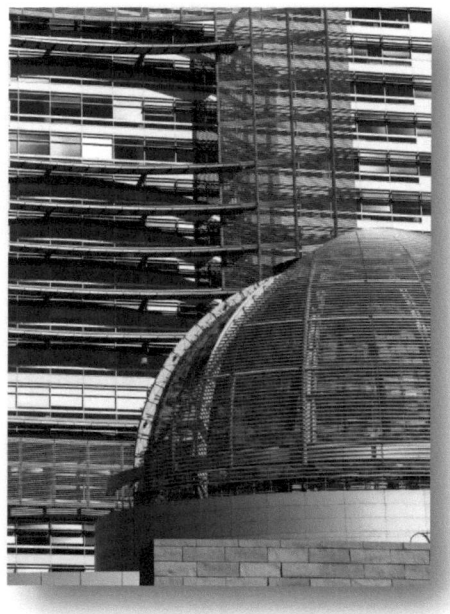

The Photographer's Quick Guide to Earning Money From Your Photos

Urban landscapes also make interesting photos, where buildings of widely differing ages and styles are hard against each other, or surprising touches of color stand out in an otherwise plain area.

Urban and industrial photography can be about art pieces, or it can be about more commercial shots, either to sell as stock photography, or to sell to businesses, local Chambers of Commerce, Tourist Bureaus and similar.

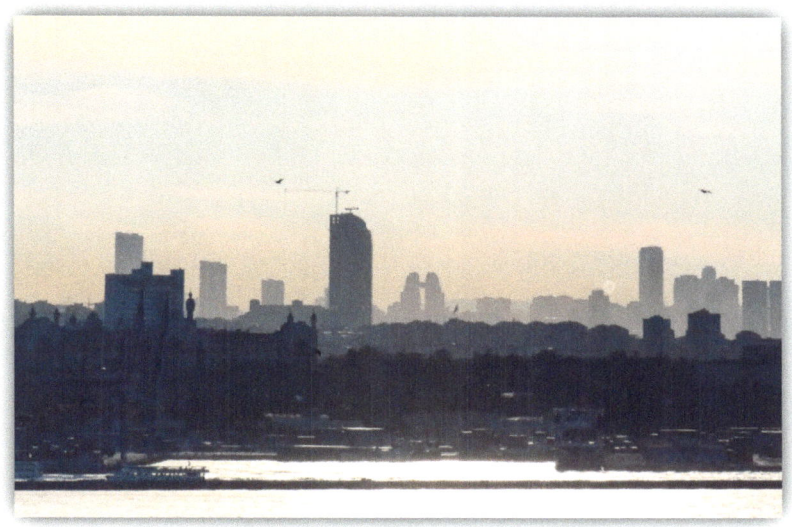

This shot captures the Port in Istanbul, at dawn, seen across the water as the early light just starts to pick out the detail.

KIM LAMBERT

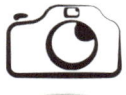

6. **Holiday Themed Pictures (see Book 7 in this series)**

There is always a market for holiday themed pictures ! There are lots of holidays throughout the year (Christmas, Valentine's Day, Easter, Mother's Day, Father's Day, Halloween (pumpkins example below), Thanksgiving etc etc), all of which have traditional activities and imagery associated with them. Every year, graphic artists are looking for new pictures to use in creating advertising, web banners and other items related to those holidays.

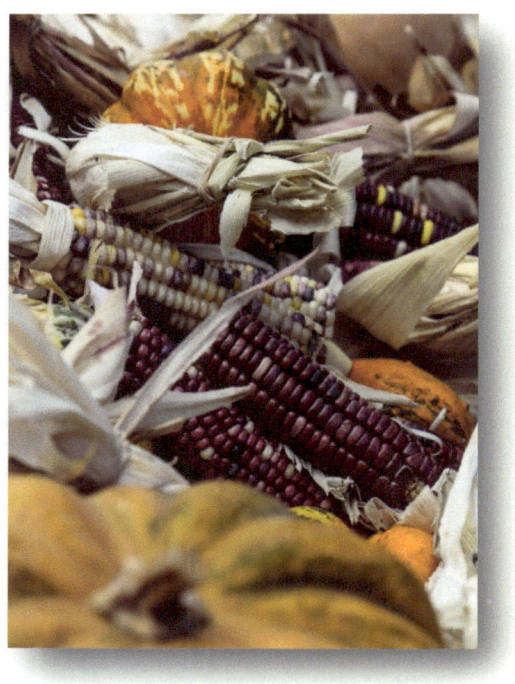

The Photographer's Quick Guide to Earning Money From Your Photos

So, even though pictures relating to one holiday will only sell around that time each year, if you have a portfolio of pictures which are themed around different holidays, something will be selling all year. Again, the trick in making a 'money worthy' picture is to make it different enough to stand out from others photos – new angles, new ways of presenting things, decorations made out of unusual materials, pictures with a bit of comedy to them, anything that is not 'just another cute Christmas tree' or the like.

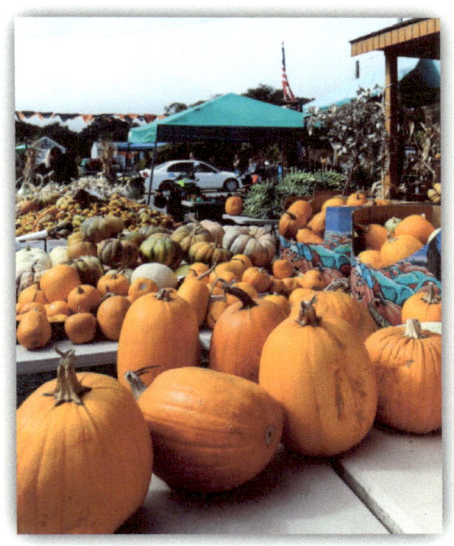

If you can make the holiday image seem perfect – clean, bright, and capturing 'essence of holiday' then it will sell.

KIM LAMBERT

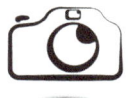

7. **Pictures of People – in all Aspects of Life and Emotion (see Book 8 in this series)**

Portraits, as mentioned earlier, are just one aspect of photographing people. Portraits are most frequently quite structured, and aimed at capturing the person by themselves. Pictures of people can cover a huge range though – groups of people engaged in activities, children enjoying getting messy, people playing with animals, doing sports – endless possibility.

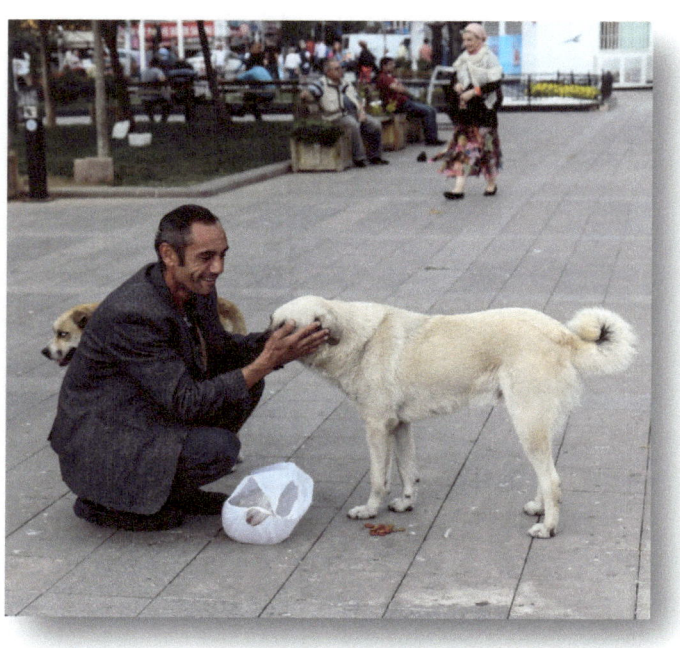

The Photographer's Quick Guide to Earning Money From Your Photos

Of particular interest are pictures that capture emotions – not just happiness or serenity (which is what standard portraits usually go for) – advertisers in particular look for photos they can use which show people looking sad, shocked, amazed, horrified, scared, tired, sick, sneezing etc. they use those photos to emphasize the problems that the products being advertised are supposed to solve.

So there is a quite profitable market in taking pictures of people doing things that they do not normally like to be photographed doing!

Remember to get a signed 'model release' (an agreement that the person is happy for you to sell pictures of them) from anyone you photograph where you will sell the picture. Stock photo sites will usually have a clear explanation of what they expect in a model release. (there are some types of shot that you can sell as 'editorial' without a model release)

Some of the best selling stock photos are of people having a good time – laughing around a dinner table with a glass of wine, hugging and smiling, that sort of thing.

But pictures of people do not have to be all beautiful people either, any more than they have to be of beautiful emotions or expressions. Again, there is demand for pictures of people of all ages, and characteristics, beautiful to not so beautiful – interesting wrinkled and aged faces also can sell well.

KIM LAMBERT

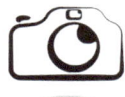

8. Food Photos (see Book 9 in this series)

Food (and wine) photos are always popular (how many people do you know who buy cookbooks just to look at the pictures, or who post pictures of what the eat at restaurants, on FaceBook?) and there are many options for selling them.

Stock photography sites are always looking for good food photos, food photos are also a key part of travel advertising, and of local tourist advertising. Local restaurants may be interested in getting photos of their food to display on their premises, and framed or mounted food pictures are often sold in kitchen ware shops or interior decoration shops as well. They also sell well at local markets or craft chops in many areas.

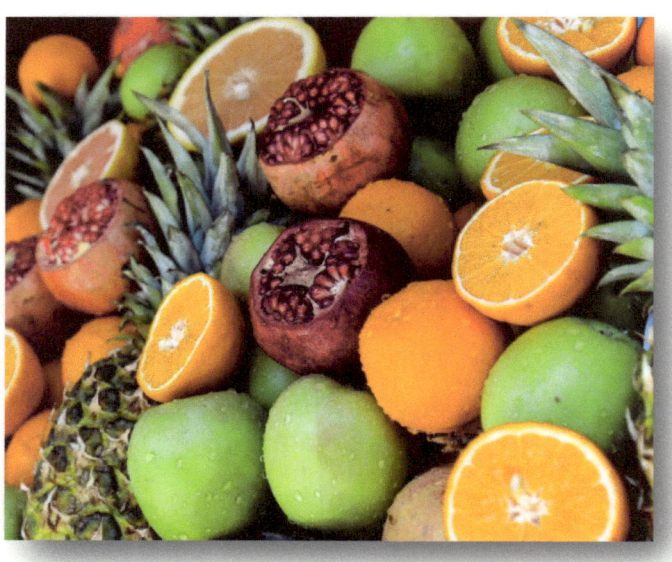

The Photographer's Quick Guide to Earning Money From Your Photos

If you are in a food shop or restaurant, and there is food worth photographing, ask the shop staff if they mind – not only do they usually not mind, but they will often go out of their way to give you better things to photograph, or better angles to get to them!

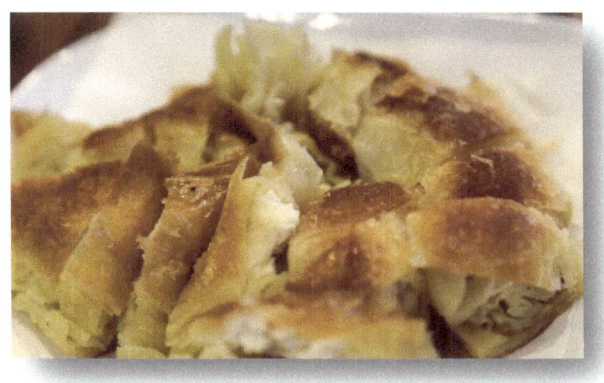

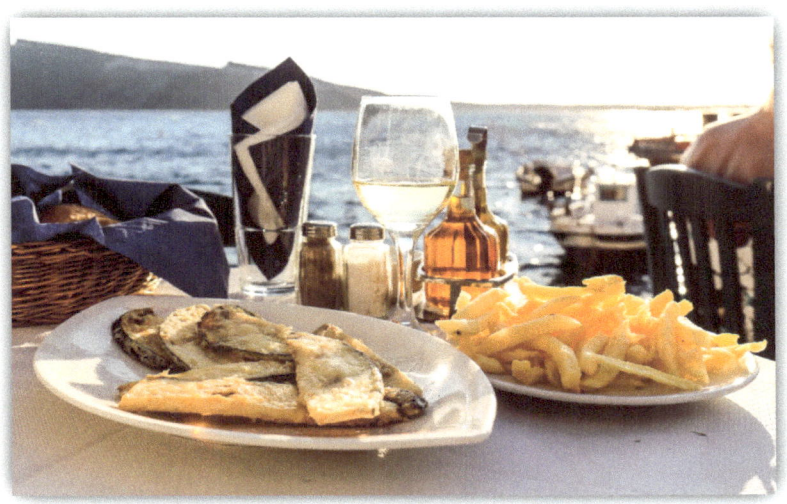

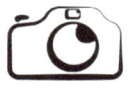

9. Themed groups of photos for books (see Book 10 in this series)

With the ability to self publish through various online sites, including Amazon.com's Createspace system, it has become relatively easy to put together, and sell, books which are primarily pictorial in nature – those books we would have traditionally referred to as 'coffee table" books.

Where in the days of traditional publishing, such books were expensive to publish, and hence difficult to get publisher to agree to do, today's print-on-demand capability means that there is no up-front cost – so you can choose to create and publish any book you wish. If you just want to create books of your pictures, but don't want to have to learn how to do the publishing bit, there are plenty of businesses (like mine – see the Resources List at Chapter 7 of this book for more information) which will help you do that part.

Photographic travel books are always saleable – people love to travel vicariously – it's a way to 'feel like you are there' even if you can't afford it.

That doesn't mean that you need to travel far to make such a book – because there are people who would like to travel to your home area, or places nearby. Try a partnership with someone who loves to write about travel, or just loves to write, and you can create a book which is primarily pictorial on any topic.

The Photographer's Quick Guide to Earning Money From Your Photos

That can be children's books (things like an animal alphabet, for example), or books about craft or jewelry – anything where the subject lends itself to lots of pictures. It could be dogs, or horses – books on animals are always popular!

As an example, here are a couple of pictures of cats from my upcoming book "Street Cats Of The World"

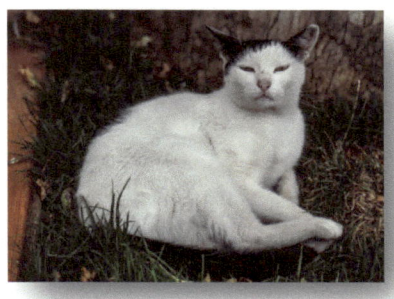

The white cat was at an outdoor café in Istanbul, and the tabby kitten below on the back street of an ancient town on Santorini.

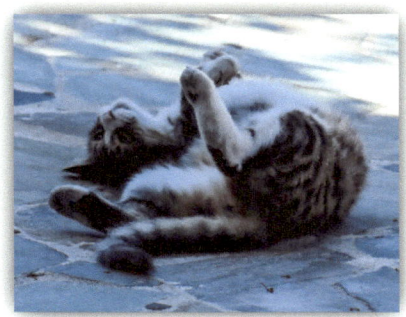

You can also sometimes sell pictures to others who are publishing books – often travel or regional information books – this takes a bit more research and work to sell yourself, but can be quite lucrative.

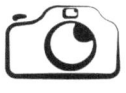

10. Photos specifically taken to be sold as stock photos (see Book 12 in this series)

Taking pictures specifically for stock photos is an art in itself – you have to stop thinking of the picture in a frame on the wall, and think of it as a component, or background, that a graphic designer may use to create something new. Because of how stock photos are used, there are some constraints (like not having brand names visible on objects in them, and having model release forms for people in your pictures), but there are also some amazing things that you can do.

Graphic designers need backgrounds – so stock photography sites like pictures of plain wooden floors, fabric textures, soft focus interesting blurs and other things like that. So, your 'mistakes' may actually be saleable!

All the usual things apply, as far as making a picture 'money worthy', but the range of things that you can photograph is enormous – your house is a treasure trove of ordinary objects that would make great stock photos – things like kitchen implements or vases of flowers.

But the best way to start, is just to start…. Every time you see an advertisement, or a webpage, look at the graphic elements, and consider where those pictures came from – you will begin to rapidly get ideas for what you could photograph to sell as stock photos.

The Photographer's Quick Guide to Earning Money From Your Photos

Here is an example of one of my shots that was accepted by a stock photo site as a background. It was a classic mistake shot – an accidental push of the button as I walked along, capturing a blur of grass and earth as I moved. It's the sort of thing you probably delete – so think again and keep things like this !

There are some great courses around to teach you how to do stock photography well. If you are interested in learning a lot more about taking photos just for stock photography (even more detail than I cover in book 12 of this series!), and improving your photography skills as you do, you will be interested in the material at the Breakfast Stock Club, on the Photographers Life website, at Http://www.thephotographerslife.com/bsc/kl/ . Also see the Resources List at Chapter 7 of this book for more information.

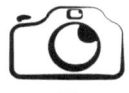

11. Photos taken to create T-shirt or clothing designs (see Book 12 in this series)

These days everyone wears T-shirts and Hoodies with designs of some kind on them. Many of those are computer or hand drawn graphic art, but many are also pictures, or pictures that have been modified in Photoshop or similar, often with text added. Shirts are so popular that there are sites online which are just about creating and selling shirts in various ways, plus many of the 'artists market' type sites also have shirts as one of the possible product sets. The profit from these can be quite good, and they are easy – you do the design and list it, the sites do the sales, manufacture and shipping, then pay you a percentage of the sale price.

Depending on how the site manufactures its shirts, you may need to use Photoshop or similar to post process your picture towards a line drawing, or other treatment, as some screen printing methods can only deal with 10 colors (color includes shades of grey....)You can take pictures specifically for shirts – things like a cute picture of a dog of a specific breed, and add the text "I Love Spaniels" (or whatever kind of dog it is) - there will always be buyers for shirts like that.

Just do some research and pick a target group of people who are obsessively passionate about a particular thing.

The Photographer's Quick Guide to Earning Money From Your Photos

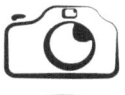

12. Photos specifically taken as creative art (see Book 11 in this series)

If you like to see your work up on the wall in a frame, then there are a number of options for where to sell (as mentioned in Chapter 1).

If you are taking pictures specifically aimed at the fine art market, you will need to be very careful with your photographic quality, and really work at finding unusual and interesting angles on your subjects, so as to make your work stand out from that of other photographers.

If you find that you often see the world around you as full of unusual angles on things, and that your shots are often too 'arty' to sell well as stock images, then this is a good niche for you.

The other aspect of creative art photography is where you specifically take pictures which are structured so that prints can be used for making imitation antique pictures, or used in decoupage or scrapbooking. This also allows a very different view on the world and can be lots of fun.

Photos framed and sold through galleries as exclusive fine art can command quite high prices, so if you have an eye for that sort of thing, and relatively high quality camera equipment, this is a good niche to explore.

Here are a couple of examples of the sort of pictures that could be marketed as fine art.

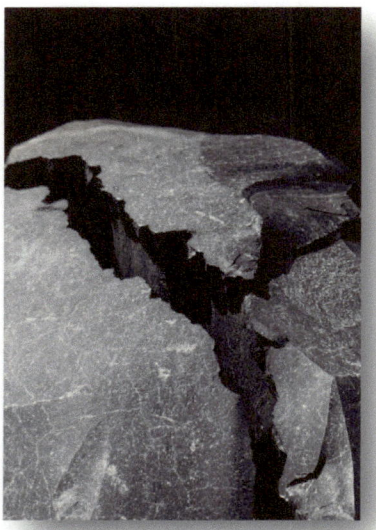

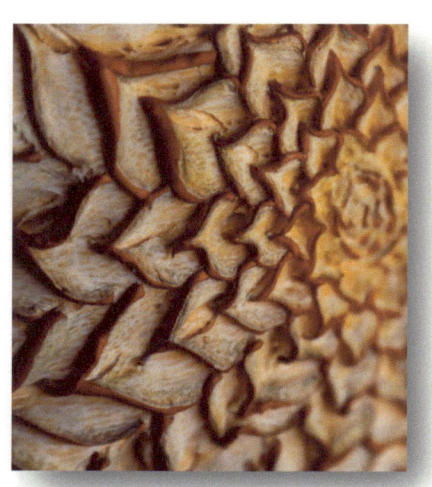

Chapter 5 – Debunking Common Myths About Making Money From Photography

There are many beliefs that are commonly held about whether or not you can make money from photography – most of them date from the era of film cameras, and are now not really valid anymore.

These myths persist, however, and are repeated by those who have not investigated what is really possible.

In this Chapter we look at a few of them, and what the current day truth of the matter is.

You will probably find that you have been told a few, if not all, of these, by the people around you.

Choose to not believe them! Go out and earn from your photography instead.

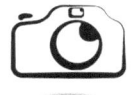

1. Myth 1: You need lots of highly expensive equipment

Whilst it is certainly true that more expensive, higher quality equipment will make it easier to get high quality results, the key factor in taking a good photo is **YOU**.

No amount of expensive equipment will make up for bad framing, uninteresting angles and lack of attention to detail.

Modern digital cameras have amazing capabilities for the money, and so long as you pick a camera that suits the style of photography you want to do, and is of at least reasonable quality, you will be able to take great pictures.

In addition, the ability to adjust and fix a wide range of things in post-processing ensures that you can deal with minor challenges that your equipment may present.

So – start out with what you can afford, or what you already have, and only upgrade when you really want to – using the money that you have already earned from your photos, to buy your new camera!

The Photographer's Quick Guide to Earning Money From Your Photos

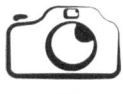

2. Myth 2: You need many years of experience

Whilst experience / practice will undoubtedly make your work improve (so long as you choose to consciously keep on learning), it is not necessary to start making money from your photography.

Again, if a person does not see the interesting angles, pay attention to details, get the framing right and think about their lighting and timing, then no amount of experience will improve their photos.

Equally, if you DO pay attention to those things, from the start, you will be able to create amazing pictures very rapidly – and your technique will then improve over time.

Inexperience is not a barrier to creative thinking, or vision. Go out and try, and when you submit pictures to a stock site, and they are rejected,, they will tell you why, and you can learn, and improve your work – or…. your pictures may be accepted first try!

Similarly, if people comment on your work, every comment is an opportunity to see things through a potential buyers eyes, and learn what to do to tempt more people to purchase your work.

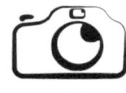

3. Myth 3: The only way to earn money from photos is to have a traditional professional photography business

This has not been true for over a century, if it ever was. From the earliest days of publications like National Geographic, there have been photographers who made money from their photos, by travelling, or capturing the interesting characteristics of their local scenery or people.

The 'traditional professional photography business' is a concept born of an era when film cameras and film and processing were expensive, and most small towns would have one photographer, who ran a business that dealt in all kinds of photographic work.

This was partly driven by costs, but also by available market – until the advent of digital cameras, and the internet, it was difficult to market your work to a wide audience, so competition for customers could be tough.

Not any more – everyone in the world is now your potential customer – and there is someone out there who wants to buy what you want to photograph – you just need to find the best way to reach them!

The Photographer's Quick Guide to Earning Money From Your Photos

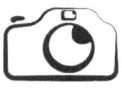

4. Myth 4: Only photos of beautiful things can make money

This is a really interesting concept – we think of art as being about capturing beauty – and, whilst it very much can be, it is also about capturing the world as it is. So pictures of graffiti can be as interesting as pictures of a beautiful flower.

Stock photography sites, in particular, are happy to see pictures of trash, or people making 'horrible faces', of children with mud all over them and other things that are not typically considered 'beautiful'.

Why ?

Because if you want to advertise facial tissues, you probably want a picture of a person sneezing.

If you want to advertise a garden clean up service, you probably want a picture of trash to illustrate what it is you get rid of...

There are hundreds of examples like this, and graphic artists creating advertisements for those companies go to stock photo sites to find images to use. So – look around you, and start to photograph things that are not 'pretty' but may very well make you money!

Here is an example of a trash photo that could be useful – it's a broken tennis ball, dropped on the pine leaves in a recreation park – a really good example of what we want to avoid, that could be used in something like 'protect your park' advertising.

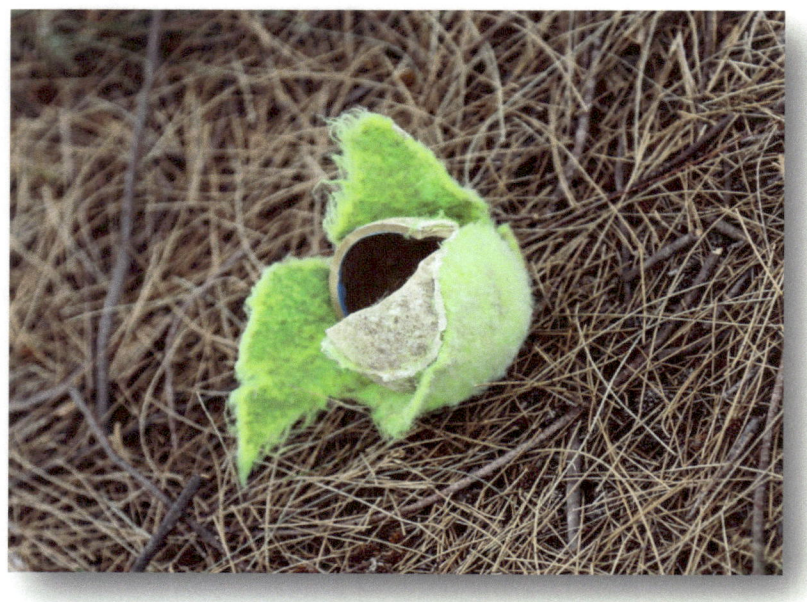

Chapter 6 – Your Action Plan

OK, Now we have had a look at all of the possibilities, are you ready to get started on your money making photographic journey?

Don't hesitate, you CAN do it. (and, depending on what you choose to do, you'll find that other books in this series can help you develop your work further.)

In just 8 steps, you can go from start to pictures out there, selling.

Those 8 steps are:
1. Choose a type of photography that suits your personal interests
2. Choose how you want to sell
3. Decide what equipment changes you want or need to make (if any)
4. Decide what post processing and photo library management software you will use
5. See if you already have photos that you can start to sell now
6. Take your first 'targeted photos'
7. Prepare your first batch of photos for sale
8. Submit them for sale

Here is some more detail about each step.

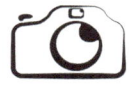

1. Choose a type of photography that suits your personal interests

You won't like taking photos of things you are not interested in, and if you are not enjoying yourself, you won't take good pictures. So start by writing a list of the things you most enjoy doing, and photographing. Then pick the thing on that list that most 'grabs' you when you think about it. Let's start from there! Does that line up with any of the photography types in Chapter 4 ?

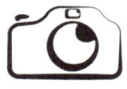

2. Choose how you want to sell

Go back to Chapter 2 and read through it again. Does any one place to sell really appeal to you, or suit your location or lifestyle ? Or have you thought of something completely different, after considering these options ? Where you choose first is less important than that you do choose one to start with. Now think about what sort of pictures and presentation of pictures you will need to sell through that channel.

The Photographer's Quick Guide to Earning Money From Your Photos

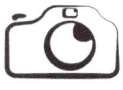

3. Decide what equipment changes you want or need to make (if any)

Are you happy with the camera equipment that you have ? can it produce high enough photographic quality pictures to suit the sales channel that you have chosen? Is it convenient for taking the type of pictures that you want to take ? If you did change it, what would you want ? can you afford it now, or do you have to wait? Make a choice, and act on it!

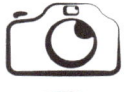

4. Decide what post processing and photo library management software you will use

Do you have any software now ? Do you have a storage and cataloguing system for your photos now (manual or software) ? If you do have post processing software, do you know how to use it ? Pick something (see list in Chapter 7) and spend a bit of time learning how to use it. There are some good courses listed in Chapter 7 as well.

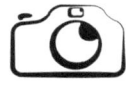

5. See if you already have photos that you can start to sell now

Now that you know what sort of pictures you want to sell, and where you want to sell them, go back through your picture collection and see what you have already that might work. Are those pictures of good enough quality ? can you see how you will use your new-found post-processing skills to improve them ? Use those pictures to practice, and prepare them for sale, while you also think about where you are going to take new pictures, specifically with your aim in mind.

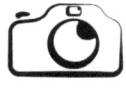

6. Take your first 'targeted photos'

OK, so now you have a type of picture in mind, a sales channel chosen, and have practiced your picture prep using existing shots. Now – where is the best place to take some pictures specifically for your new money earning approach ? This might be your kitchen table, if you are taking stock photos of household objects, or it could be your local dog club. Choose a location, and go try taking some shots!

The Photographer's Quick Guide to Earning Money From Your Photos

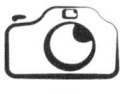

7. Prepare your first batch of photos for sale

OK, let's have a look at those pictures you just took! Did they turn out like you wanted ? Or did some of those background features, that the brain edits out, sneak in ? Is the lighting right ? are they sharply in focus ? have a play with them in your post processing software (I personally use both Adobe Photoshop and Adobe Lightroom). Did you improve them ? Consider if they are better than the ones you found in your current collection, then choose 6 to 10 that you will use for your first batch to sell. If you are selling for stock, make sure that they meet the guidelines of the site you will submit to. If you are selling prints, now is the time to arrange good quality printing.

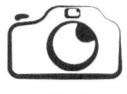

8. Submit them for sale

If you are selling online, deep breath, upload, add metadata information and press submit! If you are selling physical prints, off you go to the shop, gallery or market, and see how they respond – Good Luck!

KIM LAMBERT

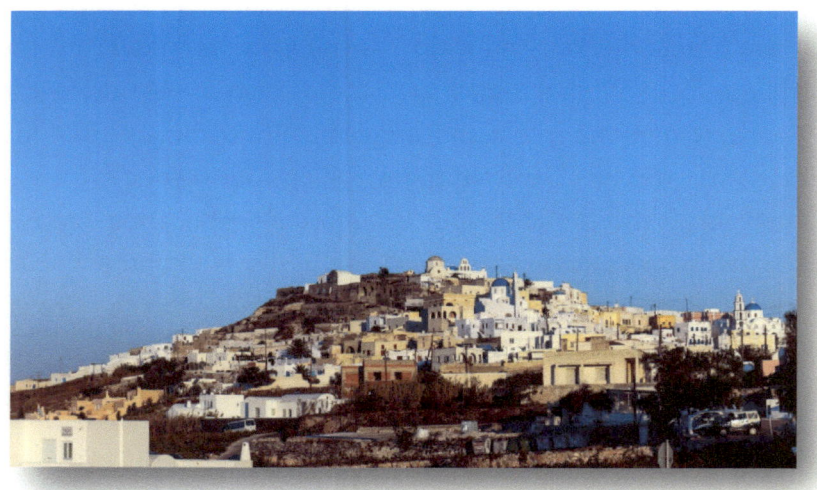

Chapter 7 – Resource Lists

Here are some resources for you, as mentioned at various points in the book.

Stock photography sites
- Bigstock - http://www.bigstockphoto.com/
- Shutterstock - http://www.shutterstock.com/
- iStock - http://www.istockphoto.com/
- ThinkStock - http://www.thinkstockphotos.com
- Dreamstime - http://www.dreamstime.com/
- 123RF - http://www.123rf.com/
- Veer - http://www.veer.com/
- Alamy - http://www.alamy.com
- Fotolia - http://fotolia.com/
- Graphicstock - http://www.graphicstock.com/
- Getty Images - http://www.gettyimages.com.au/
- Macrografiks - https://macrografiks.com/ (macro photo specific)
- CanStock Photo - http://www.canstockphoto.com/

KIM LAMBERT

Artist's Market style sites

- Redbubble - www.redbubble.com

    (the author's redbubble portfolio is at http://www.redbubble.com/people/kyriiahn/portfolio)

- 500px - http://500px.com/ (the authors 500px portfolio is at - http://kimlambert.500px.com/#/0)

T-shirt specific sites

- Teespring - http://www.teespring.com/
- Redbubbles Tshirt shop –

    http://www.redbubble.com/shop/t-shirts?ref=home_leftnav

Book production sites

- Createspace – http://www.createspace.com
- Kindle – http://kdp.amazon.com
- Smashwords - http://www.smashwords.com/
- Blurb - http://www.blurb.com

    (the authors books on blurb are at - http://www.blurb.com/user/Kriian)

- Lulu - http://www.lulu.com/
- Thorpe-Bowker ebook services (this is the same company where you buy ISBNs if you want to self allocate) - https://www.myidentifiers.com.au/bowker_ebook_solutions

There are more, but that is a start.

The Photographer's Quick Guide to Earning Money From Your Photos

Craft sales sites

- Etsy - http://www.etsy.com/

- Ebay – http://www.ebay.com

There are others, but these are by far the biggest marketplaces online. Local craft shops abound – check out your local area to find some.

Software products

- Adobe – Adobe have been the leaders in image management and manipulation software for decades – originally for graphic designers, then for web designers and photographers, now for app builders and movie makers too. The primary products that you will want to use as a photographer are Adobe Photoshop, and Adobe Lightroom. Previously these were quite expensive, but you can now get them as part of a 'creative cloud' membership, for anywhere from $10 to $90 a month, depending on how many applications you want (the high end membership gives you access to about 40 applications!) http://www.adobe.com/creativecloud

- Gimp – is an Open source application which is approximately the equivalent of Photoshop, and is well regarded for its capabilities. http://www.gimp.org

- Digikam – An open source integrated photo management suite, which gives you the sort of cataloguing capability that Adobe Lightroom does (features are never exactly equivalent) - http://www.digikam.org

- Rawtherapy – Specifically for processing images in RAW format, it has Lightroom like capabilities. - Http://www.rawtherapy.com

Camera guides information sites

There are a lot of sites on the Internet which provide reviews and commentary on various camera models and lenses. Here are a few to get you started when you are considering new equipment.

- Digital Photography Review - http://www.dpreview.com
- Camera Labs - http://www.cameralabs.com/
- Digital Camera Review – http://www.digitalcamerareview.com/
- Photo Review - http://www.photoreview.com.au/

Courses to learn more about various photography types in depth

There are lots of courses you can take to improve your photography, either online or at your local community college or similar.

A good site to learn about various photography types is

- *Digital Photography School* - http://digital-photography-school.com/ They have lots of information and a fairly active community of people interacting. They are primarily focused on general photography education, rather than being specifically focused on how to earn money from photography.

The Photographer's Quick Guide to Earning Money From Your Photos

For very in-depth, detailed courses on earning money from your photography of different types

- *The Photographer's Life* - This site is part of a group of educational sites with a specific focus on earning money in different fields, and provides very, very comprehensive information on each approach, with a huge number of tutorials and support available to members of their programs.

    They have a detailed, on-line course all about how to Turn Your Pictures into Cash, the information is at

    http://www.thephotographerslife.com/ph4/kl/

    If you are interested in learning a lot more about taking photos just for stock photography (even more detail than I cover in book 12 of this series!), and improving your photography skills as you do, see the Breakfast Stock Club, on the Photographers Life website, at Http://www.thephotographerslife.com/bsc/kl/

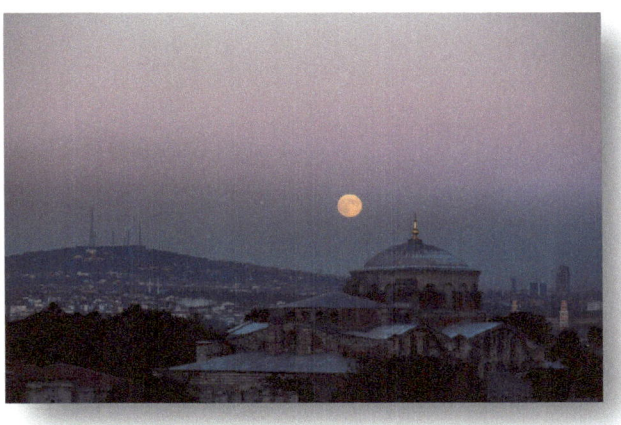

KIM LAMBERT

Now......
Go and take Wonderful Photographs and enjoy the rewards that follow !

The Photographer's Quick Guide to Earning Money From Your Photos

Look out for further titles in The "Photographer's Quick Guide.." Series

By Kim Lambert

Taking Beautiful Portraits

Taking Spectacular Travel photos

Capturing Amazing Landscapes

Getting Up Close – Macro Photos

Urban and Industrial Photography

Pictures with a Holiday Theme

Taking Great Pictures of People

Taking Gorgeous Food Photos

Publishing Books with Your Pictures

Finding Local Places to Sell Your Prints

Selling Your Photos Online

Tying it all Together: Actively Marketing Your Photography

All Books available from all Amazon sites and other book stores, and available for Kindle too!.

KIM LAMBERT

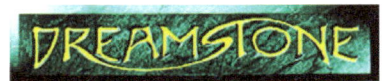

Other Books from Dreamstone Publishing

Dreamstone publishes books in a wide variety of categories Please visit us at www.dreamstone.com.au – here are some of our other books:-

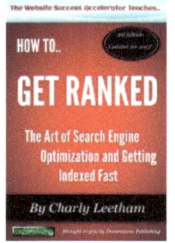

Get Ranked - The Art of Search Engine Optimisation and Getting Indexed Fast (The Website Success Accelerator Teaches....) *By Charly Leetham*

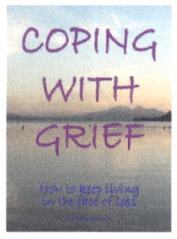

Coping With Grief

By Penny Clements

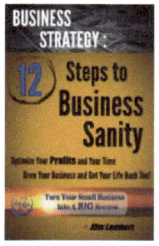

Business Strategy : 12 Steps to Business Sanity How to Optimize Your Profits and Your Time, Grow Your Business and Get Your Life Back Too!

By Kim Lambert

The Photographer's Quick Guide to Earning Money From Your Photos

ABOUT THE AUTHOR

Kim Lambert is an author, photographer (see a lot more about her photographic history in the Foreword to this book), business woman and entrepreneur, with a background ranging from Technical Management and Development in the computing field to cooking and sewing as part of a medieval recreation group, and making theatrical costumes.

She writes photography books and cookbooks for fun (as a bit of a change from business books!) and also helps others publish their books (regardless of topic!). She lives near Canberra, Australia, and travels as often as possible, always with a camera in her hand.

All of the pictures in this book (except the portrait of her at the start of the book) are her work, mostly from the 2010 to 2014 period.

If you are interested in obtaining a print, or licensing the use of, any of these images, or would like to see more of her work, please contact here through the publisher of this book on info@dreamstone.com.au

She is also available for interviews, or articles through the same contact.

www.ingramcontent.com/pod-product-compliance
Lightning Source LLC
Chambersburg PA
CBHW040220220526
45473CB00001B/64